The Mind of an Activist—James Connolly

LIBRARY
FLORIDA STATE UNIVERSITY
TALLAHASSEE, FLORIDA

The Mind of an Activist—
James Connolly

The centenary lecture delivered on 10 May 1968 under the auspices of the Irish Congress of Trade Unions, in Liberty Hall

OWEN DUDLEY EDWARDS

I continued to listen to their talk and there was mention continually of somebody named Connolly. Connolly says so and so. Connolly does not agree with that. Connolly's point of view is this, and so on. Then when I had an opportunity I asked who was this Connolly. 'He is a very smart fellow,' I was told. 'Where does he come from?' 'From Edinburgh.' 'And what is he?' 'Just a labourer.' 'A labourer?' said I. 'How could a labourer know all these things?' 'He went to the National Library and he studied.' This was not very convincing to me. I could not understand how a labourer should be so important as all that. The labourers I was acquainted with were people who drifted around the roads and took up casual jobs and were almost entirely illiterate. However, I had to accept what was stated.

William O'Brien,
Forth the Banners Go

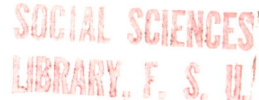

GILL AND MACMILLAN

Published by
GILL AND MACMILLAN LTD
2 Belvedere Place
Dublin 1

and in London through association with the
MACMILLAN
Group of Publishing Companies

© Owen Dudley Edwards 1971

7171 0533 4

Cover design by Hilliard Hayden

Printing history:
10 9 8 7 6 5 4 3 2 1

Printed and bound in the Republic of Ireland by
Cahill and Co. Limited, Dublin 8

To the memory of
Noel Hartnett
Disciple of Connolly
Advocate of the underman
Crusader for Irish Socialism

Contents

	Prefatory Note	ix
1	Connolly's World	1
2	Connolly and Catholicism	28
3	The Problem of the Easter Week Rising	65
4	The Lost Heir	84
5	Connolly and Ourselves	106
	Epilogue: Connolly 1968 and 1971	109
	Notes	114

Prefatory Note

The present text is based on a lecture given by me in honour of the birth of James Connolly. The lecture was delivered at Liberty Hall on Friday 10 May 1968 under the auspices of the Irish Congress of Trade Unions. It was tape-recorded, and I have employed the recording in the preparation of these pages. I have also drawn on a sketch of the mind of Connolly which I prepared for the *Irish Times* centenary supplement, which appeared on 5 June 1968. I have included several additional points in the light of criticisms of the original lecture which were made to me. In a few instances I have deleted material which I felt to be appropriate to the circumstances of the original lecture but which a printed version would render somewhat out of place. Any point of contemporary significance which was then made by me, and which I have now deleted, is none the less to be regarded as my view now as then. I have tried to preserve something of the atmosphere of a lecture, and it will probably be agreed that at least I have preserved the impression of a lecture running well over its allotted time. The transition from an oral to a written presentation presents many serious problems, and I have retained a more discursive style than is customary with printed studies. I hope the reader will not find this too irritating, and that he will not be inordinately repelled by some degree of repetition in the points made, which I regard as a major necessity in the structure of a lecture.

It was as a historian that I was asked to speak on this occasion, but the Irish Congress of Trade Unions, which paid me this signal honour, recognised that I believed in approaching the subject with more than the historian's commitment. On an academic level, it was also necessary to examine Connolly from the standpoint of the political scientist, including the political scientist's sense of the relevance of his subject to the present. I also spoke as a Socialist and as a Catholic; and in my position as both I could not do justice to such an occasion without indicating what Connolly had given to both faiths. I am bound to say that I do not regard this paper as a departure from history; if we ignore what Connolly means to us we are unlikely to discover what he meant in the context of his own times. It is of course true, as Connolly would be the first to warn us, that concentration on a single individual can weaken our historical sense. I would hope, however, that concentration on Connolly can open our minds to his own times, from which he cannot be cut away, and to our times, in which we have so much to learn from him. Irishmen are growing increasingly conscious of our imprisonment by the past, and it is unquestionable that a narrow absorption in our past can lead to introversion, to arid conservatism and to intellectual blinkers. On the other hand, failure to turn to the past must deprive us of any depth in our approach to our own problems today.

My grateful thanks are due to the Irish Congress of Trade Unions for having asked me to undertake this lecture, and I would like to express my appreciation of the kind words of the then President, the late John Conroy, who was in the chair during the lecture. Mr James Dunne, his successor, gave me all the reward I could wish in his most moving, and far too generous, speech of thanks on the same occasion. Even deeper must go my gratitude to Mr Donal Nevin, the Assistant General Secretary, who did everything possible to facilitate my work in giving the address; it was a very great privilege to co-operate with him on this matter, conscious as I am that he is a scholar of much greater distinction on Connolly than I can claim to be.

In the preparation of this lecture I owe, as always, the greatest of debts to Dr Patrick Henchy, Director of the National Library of Ireland, for his kindness, his unfailing assistance and his most rewarding suggestions. Mr Ailfrid Mac Lochlainn, Keeper of Printed Books in the same institution, was most helpful in drawing my attention to important source material and in making some valuable criticisms of the lecture. Father Thomas Counihan, S.J., a veteran of the labour movement and a benign and thought-provoking friend and mentor of mine for many years, has been unfailing in suggestions, from which my revision has benefited greatly; to him also I owe the loan of a very rare pamphlet. My colleagues on the *Irish Times* were an inspiration, as always, in suggestions and criticisms: I would particularly like to thank Mr Douglas Gageby (who is responsible for my education on the Belfast labour movement), Mr Donal Foley, Mr Liam Mac Gabhann, Mr Donal O'Donovan, Mr John Horgan, Mr James Downey and Mr Fergus Pyle. Some of them may be surprised by this tribute: one thing that makes

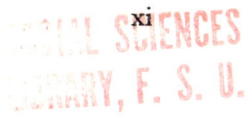

them such good teachers is that they don't know when they are teaching. I received further stimulus for my lecture by a very helpful conversation with my father, Professor R. Dudley Edwards, shortly before it. My friend Dr George Jeffares presented me with a most useful pamphlet, and has enabled me to have some helpful exchanges of ideas with him. Mr C. Desmond Greaves, who visited me in Aberdeen, opened his vast store of knowledge of Connolly and his times to me in a discourse sparkling with information and entertainment. It will also be evident how much I owe to Mr Aindreas Ó Gallchoir, of Telefís Éireann, who taught me so much when I was his assistant on his 1916 films. Miss P. J. Storey, former secretary in the Department of History at the University of Edinburgh, did much to bring the final text of this lecture into existence. My gratitude to my wife, and my friends Mr and Mrs Michael Williams, is due for that reassurance which makes any such enterprise possible.

Any criticisms of the lecture are of course to be made against myself, and not to these benefactors.

Owen Dudley Edwards

Department of History,
University of Edinburgh
New Year's Day, 1969

In the interval between the preparation of this work for the press in early 1969, and the present time, a delay occurred for which the publisher, Mr Michael Gill, is entirely responsible. His crime lay in luring me into writing a volume on the origins of the Northern Ireland crisis, in the course of which I obtained some startling proofs of the survival of Connolly. But the last revision to be made on the present work in the light of some excellent points raised by Professor Patrick Lynch, and by Mr Hubert Mahony of Gill and Macmillan had to be set aside until the other, larger, and more urgently required book was finished, and the requirements of academic life delayed that revisal still further. In making it now, I have sought to preserve the tone and atmosphere of 1968, and to retain my remarks within that framework. The essay was, after all, an outgrowth of the commemorative celebrations of 1966–68, not of the Irish upheavals of 1969–71, and were I to allow for the change of atmosphere the result would make it appear that the lecture lasted three years: I am garrulous enough as it is. But I have added a brief epilogue embodying some reflections on my theme in the light of what has happened since I placed my text aside. In doing so I have much pleasure in thanking Professor Lynch and Mr Mahony.

I must also record my gratitude to my colleague in the University of Edinburgh, Professor Victor Kiernan, for the loan of a most helpful work, and for very stimulating comment on Connolly and Marxism in general. Professor George Shepperson, of the same institution, has as always been a fund of ideas and encouragement for me. Mr T. F. Cole, also an Edinburgh colleague, supplied a translation from the German of biographical material relevant to Wilhelm Hohoff; his characteristic good nature in so doing at very short notice was an inspiration in itself. Finally, my thanks are due to Mr Gill whose resourcefulness is as endless as his patience.

Edinburgh,   Owen Dudley Edwards
Ash Wednesday, 1971

1

Connolly's World

... because I realise that human nature is a wonderful thing, that the soul of man gives expression to strange and complex phenomena, and that no man knows what powers or possibilities for good or evil lie in humanity, I try to preserve my receptivity towards all new ideas, my tolerance towards all manifestations of social activity.[1]

This paper is not intended to embrace a brief biography of James Connolly. There is in existence an excellent life of Connolly by Desmond Greaves[2] which places his public achievements in the context of his time and writings, and which is the product of most painstaking research. There is also a remarkable sketch preserving the contemporary atmosphere, by Desmond Ryan,[3] a work which was produced not only out of what he himself had seen and heard of the generation of Connolly and of Pearse, but also from the deep knowledge of his father, W. P. Ryan, the great historian of the Irish labour movement.[4] Connolly's private life has been recorded for us in a moving narrative by his daughter Nora,[5] and his times have had many annalists, chief among them Desmond Ryan himself in his *Remembering Sion,* the

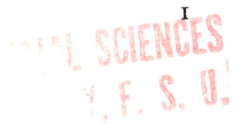

foremost memoir of the period.[6] Good studies of Connolly are in somewhat shorter supply: foremost among them is that by the late Father Lambert McKenna, S.J.[7]

Various compilations of Connolly's writings have been made, of which much the best is the three-volume selection made by Desmond Ryan. Taken together with *Labour in Ireland*[8] and some pamphlet reprints[9] these constitute an admirable introduction to Connolly's thought. But they are not in any sense comprehensive. We need and must have an edition of all of Connolly's writings, placed in chronological order of publication, and edited in the best traditions of historical scholarship. Today the Americans are bringing before the world magnificent volumes embracing all of the surviving writings of their great founders, such as Alexander Hamilton, Thomas Jefferson, Benjamin Franklin.[10] The Russians have produced a superb series embracing the totality of Lenin's output. Is it too much to ask that Ireland commemorate the most profound mind and the greatest theoretician among the founders of the modern Irish state, in this permanent form? What is required, I suggest, is the formation of an editorial board which will include certain leading historians (with at least one expert on Scottish labour history and one on American labour history), representatives of Connolly's family, interested members of the Irish labour movement, leading writers on Connolly (notably Desmond Greaves), either the Minister for Education or the Minister for Labour, representatives of the Ulster labour movement and its archival custodians, and the Director of the National Library of Ireland.

We are discovering more and more of Connolly's writings; it seems clear that the process of identification of his work in his own journals and newspapers is now likely to be speeded up; and Mr Donal Nevin has given us a very full and careful bibliography which must stand as the agenda for the commencement of editorial activity.[11]

I am particularly happy, and particularly conscious of the honour of having been asked to deliver this address on the occasion of the centenary of Connolly's birth. It is his birth, after all, which particularly demands our celebration, and the fact is one over which recent events may have led people to gloss. An important celebration was held in 1966 on the Golden Jubilee of the Easter Rising, and, productive though this was of much valuable reflection and reassessment concerning that event itself, it may have led us to focus our attention on the point that Connolly died while tending to forget that Connolly was born, lived and taught. Connolly died for his ideals; but his message is in its essence a message for men's lives, not a harbinger of death.

Connolly's death brought his teachings to the attention of a public which might otherwise never have heard of them; but simultaneously it offered an *alibi* to posterity. Since the great man was a great man, all manner of persons were quick to assert that they spoke and acted in the name of Connolly. Had he not died for an independent Ireland? And were they not the representatives of an independent Ireland? His teachings flashed before the eyes of subsequent generations, therefore, only to be dwarfed into insignificance by an official interpretation of his heritage which stressed his death alone. Connolly has been exposed to public veneration as a corpse; the object of the exercise, an object consciously held in mind, is to distract the attention from Connolly living. As early as 1924 James Larkin gave a bitter example of how quick the time-server was to wrap himself in the mantle of Connolly dead:

> The sycophant who held His Majesty's commission would bleat of his adherence to Republican principles over the grave of a Pearse or attend a military Mass in honour of a revolutionary mass-leader such as Connolly and then within the hour unctuously sign the death-warrant of a Republican.[12]

These are harsh terms, owing much of their savagery to the climate of the Civil War years. But we do not need to be so harsh. In the U.S.A. and the U.S.S.R. there are time-servers who today avow themselves to be walking in the tradition of Lincoln or of Lenin while consciously possessing nothing of their beliefs; but, again in both countries, there are also men who quite genuinely believe themselves to be in the tradition of Lincoln or Lenin, and yet have gone far from their gospels. It is indeed almost impossible in either country not to associate oneself with the national idol when engaged in political activity. In Ireland, the need to pay tribute to the men of 1916 is perhaps greater. Lincoln was a martyr and Lenin a teacher, but Connolly, after all, was both, and in some respects must be even more demanding an icon. Therefore men who quite genuinely wish to see themselves, and have others see them, as heirs to the Connolly tradition, and who yet wish to fulfil programmes of their own, are obliged to convey new impressions of Connolly.

The close student of Connolly's writings may regard such men as appealing to strange Connollys, but these men honestly regard themselves as good nationalists, are not averse to toying with some ideas of social thought, believe they stand in the realistic tradition of Connolly, represent what Connolly would do were he here today, and are essentially keepers of the Connolly legacy. A case in point comes to hand, from the celebrations of that same Golden Jubilee of the Easter Rising which commemorated Connolly's death:

> During this commemoration year [said the then Taoiseach, Mr Seán Lemass, speaking at the King's Inns] many people will ask what the leaders of 1916 would think of the Ireland of today if they could come back to view it, and some would answer this question, not perhaps always without ulterior motive, in regard to the politics of today. I think they would be astonished by the changes which have taken place in economic and social conditions, and in the outlook of our people in these matters, because these would represent developments beyond their expectations, or indeed the expectations of anybody who had been familiar only with the economic and social ideas and conditions and public attitudes to them, that prevailed everywhere fifty years ago. Even many of the views of James Connolly, revolutionary though they were considered to be in his time, seem out of date in the circumstances of today. Not only this country, but the whole world today, is, in respect of material progress, and social development, far ahead of anything that would have been considered to be likely by reasonable men at the beginning of the century.[13]

Perhaps the mental picture resultant from Mr Lemass' remarks is not so solemn as so distinguished a statesman might hope to evoke. There is a rather entertaining lack of reality about the spectacle of the leaders of the 1916 Rising looking goggle-eyed at the wonders of modern Ireland for all the world like tourists at some striking exhibit at the World's Fair. A smiling Mr Lemass discovers undreamed-of marvels to them, and James Connolly, confronted by the profundity and originality of the Dáil debates, tearfully acknowledges his ideas to be hopelessly obsolete. The signatories of the Proclamation are remorselessly confronted by their own inadequacy as they behold their first television commercial . . .

I have selected Mr Lemass as an example because it seems to me that he made in this speech a more thorough effort to come to terms with the legacy of Connolly and 1916 than is normally the case. The implication of Mr Lemass' remarks is considerably more honest than are most appeals to this tradition. Mr Lemass clearly recognises that present-day Ireland is hardly in direct succession to Connolly's teaching, and therefore in order to obtain Connolly's blessing he suggests to us that, teachings or no teachings, Connolly would endorse the set up anyway regardless of his views in his own lifetime. And as far as the Connolly who actually lived is concerned—as opposed to the presumed Connolly visitor to the Ireland of 1966—it is admitted he had little in common with our comfortable Western mid-twentieth-century way of life. But *that* Connolly is out of date.

It is somewhat ironic that Mr Lemass should have stated the advances that had been made in such materialistic terms, for Connolly has been charged by his enemies with a materialistic philosophy. As Father Lambert McKenna pointed out,[14] the charge is unjust. Connolly owed much to Marx, but this did not make him a man of materialistic values. Father McKenna could have gone farther, and exonerated Marx from that charge also: there is a considerable difference between a belief in dialectical materialism and a belief in materialistic values. In fact, much in Connolly, and to some extent in Marx, is a protest against the materialistic values of the capitalist world. It is certain that were Connolly to have seen Ireland in 1966 he would have looked at other things than the gimmickry which we have so sedulously cultivated for the past fifty years. Both he and his comrades of 1916 would have seen that the questions that still face us today are in many cases those questions with which they themselves were concerned, and to which in their writings they sought to offer answers.

Above all, it seems likely that they would have looked at the men and women whom they encountered, since it was with men and women that their primary concern was, and Connolly's primary concern above all. And if we take this as a criterion, it may be productive of both humility and understanding. It calls for humility, because whatever the extent of our material progress, we are forced to admit that the generation from which Connolly emerged was one of the most extraordinary generations in the history of the world. We in Ireland have nothing comparable today, and neither has anyone else. It may bring understanding, since an examination of that generation tells us something of the reality of Connolly's achievement, and sets him in the world of intellectual giants where he belongs. Generations such as this are but a few scattered oases in the desert of world history. Athens in the fifth century B.C., America in the era of her revolution, are two examples, and in all realism we must recognise that the generation of 1900 to 1920 in Ireland merits being placed alongside them. In literature it produced Joyce, Yeats and Synge, O'Casey and AE, and behind them an incredible degree of force for investigation and experimentation in every form of cultural activity. It was in this generation that Douglas Hyde restored the lost impulse of cultural nationalism, and disciples of Michael Cusack sought to implement his lesson that if one couldn't talk nationalism with one's mouth, one could think it with one's feet. How can we venture to compare ourselves today with the generation who sought to reconquer Ireland by means of a theatre? What is the best of our work today but painful advances in the long shadow of that generation, with all too little of its daring, of its vision, of its boundless capacity for experiment, and with virtually none of its genius? And where we have gone wrong since then is not, it seems to me, through following it, but in retreating from its challenges.

If we have failed to recapture the spirit of the giants of those days, we have utterly lost sight of the great collection of men and women of the second rank, who would themselves have deservedly won glory had they not been overshadowed by the brighter stars. In that generation one newspaper upon another emerged, debate upon debate concerning the fundamentals of man's role and objectives took place, every form of ideology was under searing discussion, a tremendous intellectual excitement seemed present. It was no time of simple leadership and slavish mass following; countless men and women supported each other on one issue, opposed each other on the next, read voraciously, criticised interminably, acted when crisis seemed to call, threw themselves without stint into whatever work they saw as their vocation. The Americans have termed it the Irish cultural renaissance, and the description is remarkably apt. It was indeed a time of renaissance, and in that time James Connolly emerged as the most remarkable political thinker of the generation.

Above all we must remember in viewing this generation that it has to be viewed as a unit, as well as being the sum of the individuals concerned. Excellent studies have been made of the men and women who played such remarkable roles in the Ireland of their time[15] but the concentration on their individual careers and achievements has perhaps tended to distract attention from the degree to which they interacted upon one another and influenced one another whether positively or negatively. The paths of so many of them crossed and recrossed in these years, and their thought was shaped and reshaped by quiet conversation, or by furious argument with one another. Their Dublin was in many respects less stratified than is the case today, though even now 'everyone knows everyone else' at least to a far greater degree than is proportionately the case for most other cultural capitals. I am suggesting a pattern of intellectual encounter in which A and B both play a part and a force of influence, however zealous A might consider himself and however much B might think his values to be fixed. We must of course remember that Connolly was something of an exception in the intellectual and cultural world of the

Dublin of his time in that, unlike most of its protagonists, he had acquired much of his political education in Scotland and in the United States. Many of his social ideas remained largely unchanged in the last twenty years of his life; many more were moulded by his experience in the American working-class movement. In terms of influence, therefore, Connolly gave much more to Dublin than he obtained from it, but Connolly was not so foolish as to fail to see a good idea or a well-turned argument when it was presented to him. Even more, he had a genius for recognising the points he held in common with a seemingly totally hostile argument. His greatest gift as a propagandist may well have been his utter lack of sectarianism, and his readiness to build on any existing common ground.[16]

It was to some extent because of the firm base of his intellectual position, and even more because of the stature of his mind and political thought, that Connolly has to be seen as a man of the foremost impact on that very remarkable generation. He counted far beyond his own circle of fellow-workers. He faced his contemporaries as the most articulate representative of the working people whose cause he upheld and on behalf of whom his writings still speak to us all. But while he never deviated from his role as an evangelist for the workers' struggle, he transformed the minds and attitudes of men whose worlds initially lay far from his. Let us remember, for example, how AE, recalling the dead leaders of 1916, found his personal identification with Connolly alone: 'Here's to you, Connolly, *my* man,/Who cast the last torch on the pile.'[17] An even more telling example is that of Pearse, whose thought Connolly transformed from a superficial cultural nationalism into a far deeper social and political nationalism. At the point when Pearse died, he had been altered from the simple Gaeliciser of his early years to an exponent of that social consciousness without which Irish nationalism is flimsy, and with which Irish nationalism can have the deepest and most significant influence at home and abroad. 'A nation', observed Pearse in his last political essay, *The Sovereign People*, written early in 1916, 'may go further and determine that all sources of wealth whatsoever are the property of the nation, that each individual shall give his service for the nation's good, and shall be adequately provided for by the nation, and that all surplus wealth shall go to the national treasury to be expended on national purposes, rather than be accumulated by private persons. . . . I do not disallow the right to private property; but I insist that all property is held subject to the national sanction.'

As we note the impact of Connolly on his generation and its nationalism, it is also vital to appreciate the external factors which enhanced the impact of his ideas. The Irish cultural renaissance was a nationalist phenomenon brought into being initially by the great nationalist force which Parnell had released, which his squabbling followers had then destroyed in the constitutionalist sphere, and which was rechannelled into countless areas of cultural, social, economic and political activity. But the intellectual quickening was, it seems to me, greatly increased by the growth of overt class conflict within this period. The increase of class-consciousness, the sharpening of class differences, the clash between labour and capital—all increased the excitement of the period and gave a greater sense of reality to those involved. Under these conditions, men who might otherwise have been dilettantes or poseurs were led to become men facing real issues and real ideas. But the presence of Connolly himself on the scene proved in many instances the critical factor in shaping this new realism. The young Joseph Plunkett, for instance, had dabbled in many areas of cultural nationalism to distract his mind from that chronic ill-health which would eventually have killed him if British bullets had not got there first. The 1913 lock-out proved a turning-point for him, and the personality of Connolly put flesh on the bones of his new ideas. Plunkett, said his sister Geraldine,[18] thought Connolly 'a most wonderful person. He was so intellectually honest. Such a big man.'

I think that phrase 'a big man' is a striking indication for us of the effect Connolly had on his contemporaries. It is curious how many of them seem to have used some such phrase as that. There seems to have been a sense of towering integrity which he transmitted. It was a mental bigness, but not an aggressive bigness. 'He was no bully nor nothing like that,' remembered James Doherty, his co-worker in the Belfast dock strike of 1911. If there is one quality in Connolly the man which shines through the intervening years it is a curious one for so courageous and unceasing a fighter—serenity. Hence Connolly's impact was destined to be enduring rather than initially cataclysmic. James Doherty made a distinction which I suspect to be as valid as regards private association as it is for public agitation: 'Larkin knew how to draw a crowd', he told me, 'but Connolly knew how to hold one.'[19]

It is all the more impressive that this sense of bigness should have impinged on so many who saw him, because physically Connolly was, of course, very small. Well he might have been. The foul air and fouler living conditions in the Cowgate of Edinburgh where he was born in 1868 did little to encourage physical survival, let alone physical growth. Indeed, the architecture and city planning of Edinburgh must have given him his first practical lesson in class division, for the city is built on two levels such that the rich, driving through the fashionable shopping centres, need not spare a glance or a thought for the dank and gloomy slums in the streets far below. Even today, after impressive campaigns of slum clearance and reallocation (from which Dublin, for all of its complacency, has much to learn), the Cowgate still stands shrouded in its darkness and subterranean grimness, contrasting with the wide sweep and attractive shop-fronts of George IV Bridge which crosses above it. It was thus that Connolly encountered capitalism's view of the place of labour. He also encountered the divisions in the working class, which capitalism encouraged and fostered: Orange against Green, Catholic against Protestant. From an early age he recognised the disruptive force of religious sectarianism in the class struggle, and his achievement in Belfast may have been at its greatest in his success at dampening it down. It was a formidable indication of the survival of the evils he fought as well as of the force of his own ideas that when a plaque was unveiled to his memory in 1968, having been erected in the Cowgate, it was stolen by Orange votaries within the week.

He worked in one ill-paid job after another, was driven through want into the British Army, and so far as we can gather, saw then in 1882 his first sight of the Ireland whence his parents had come. Thence he returned to Scotland, and the ensuing years are a continuous pattern of struggle for survival in the midst of studying, speaking, talking, learning, mastering Socialism, organising workers, and consistently coming into contact with other minds. But I think it vital to stress that Connolly's study of Socialism seems to have been made in no spirit of finding a doctrine, plumping for it, and slavishly following it up. 'A general reading of his works', observed Lambert McKenna, 'leaves on one the impression that he was very original in his thinking, that his Socialism was not a copy but an adaptation',[20] and to this I would assent provided that adaptation is not assumed to involve contradiction. Indeed, as a Socialist, one feels, Connolly seldom wasted his time in negative theorising: he was perpetually concerned to create rather than to destroy, to build bridges between men's minds rather than to create cleavages. Such a reading of his writings, from the very first of them which have survived from the 1890s to his last weeks in 1916, reveals a man who built his house of ideas on what he had received from many sources. In Connolly one sees a man who was never prepared to parrot, and who always sought to work things out for himself in the light (and not the shadow) of what he read. A receptive man, I think. A man ready to accept correction, where his writings were in question, but only after he had thought the matter over. I recall an amusing instance of this. In the journal which he edited in the United States in 1908–1909, *The Harp,* when writing of the allegation that Pope Adrian IV had in the Bull *Laudabiliter* committed Ireland to the tender mercies of King Henry II of England, Connolly said of the Bull that it was a generally accepted forgery and certainly seemed to be so. This was in the course of an article which was fairly critical of the role which the Catholic Church had played in the history of Irish nationalism. But on this point, he maintained, characteristically, that it was only fair to give the benefit of the doubt where it was possible to do so. He was in the next issue vigorously assailed by a very pious Catholic, who wrote to him saying that Pope Adrian IV had most certainly given Ireland to the English, that no question of doubt existed, and that the confirmation of the whole business by Pope Alexander III should make it quite clear. Connolly, while reasserting his readiness to denounce the authorities of the Catholic Church in full measure where justice required it, once more affirmed the need to give benefit of doubt. But after a year, he came to accept the position of his critic. He had clearly, in the interval, given the matter fresh thought once the issue had left the arena of direct, personal controversy. One sees evidence of a capacity for quiet reflection and reassessment where a lesser man would have dismissed the incident from his mind. His correspondent's arguments seemed better than his own, and hence he adopted them. The affair is a very small one, but it indicates a man who was not afraid to admit he was wrong, who neither bent with the strongest wind, nor sought to maintain a weak position after time and reflection had been allowed to work on his mind. Trivial as it is, it underlines his receptivity.

In getting to grips with Connolly's Socialism, an important point follows this argument. Some confusion seems to exist as to the nature of Connolly's sources. It is clear that the major Socialist influence on him is that of

Karl Marx. But I think we have to draw a distinction between Marxism before 1917, and Marxism since then. Marxism before 1917 was an influence of an extraordinarily important character, and recognised as such, an influence which many Socialists accepted, and many others rejected to the subsequent poverty of their social thought, but by which very few allowed themselves to be imprisoned. Marx was to these pre-1917 Socialists a most valuable stimulant; Marx helped one to do one's own thinking, but did not say rigidly what that thinking was to be. He drew up the general lines, but one had to work out the specific details for oneself. The mentality which says 'we must see what Marx would have said, and say that too', is one which seems to have little in common with the character of international Socialism as it was in Connolly's day. Where 1917 is of significance is that after that date Marxism became identified in everyone's mind with an existing state. All of our attitudes to Marxism, friendly or hostile, have become very much involved with our attitudes to that state. Our experience is therefore wholly different from Connolly's in this respect. He confronted Marxism as an idea, or as a series of ideas; we cannot separate it from the U.S.S.R. Whether one thinks this a good thing or a bad one is beside the point: the critical fact is that this is a major barrier dividing us from comprehension of Connolly, who never knew Marxism in its post-1917 condition. Inevitably the Soviet Russian experience has transformed all Marxist thought, whether a Marxist met the inspiration of that experience with acceptance or rejection or ultimately reacted with a mixture of both. And this, I think, is one of the points where we stand on the other side of a watershed and must recognise that we can only guess at what the position was before 1917. To me, at least, the pre-1917 Marxist lacked either the theoretical or the practical codification which Soviet Russia brought about. On our side of the watershed we can say that the Russian revolution and its consequences have been extremely instructive. But as a result of it, whether Marxists or not, we have lost something of the flexibility possessed by Connolly and his contemporaries in their attitudes to Marxism. And it also seems to me that Marx himself possessed something of that flexibility. He showed it, for example, in his recognition late in life that the class struggle in Russia might 'jump a stage' as indeed it was to do—the Russian experience, it will be remembered, was one in which a primarily agricultural community went under Communist rule, or, to put it in Marxist terms, there was a transition from feudalism to Communism without the normal intervening capitalist phase (there was of course some industrialism in pre-revolutionary Russia, but not enough to speak of the society as having become capitalist).

It is at least clear from Connolly's writings and those of other Socialists of his time that they did not take what in religious terms would be called a fundamentalist approach to Marxism. It is also clear, if I may make a somewhat naughty point, that Connolly was a Catholic rather than a Protestant in his approach to Marx: that is to say, he did not insist on rigid adherence to Holy Writ, in this case Marx's and Friedrich Engels' writings, but rather believed in Holy Writ assisted by tradition. He tested his book-learned knowledge in the furnace of experience; he built his Socialist armoury on conversation as well as on reading; and while we must at all times remember that he was a man of far too great intellectual strength to be blown off course by contrary ideological winds, yet in the finest sense of the words he was, like Tennyson's Ulysses, a part of all that he had met.

In our stress on Connolly's nationalism we are in danger of forgetting how much of an internationalist he really was, and how wide had been the extent of his experience. He worked in Scotland after his army experience, organising as we have said, and directing working-class militancy from there, and finally he was forced by economic necessity to accept a post in Dublin as paid organiser of the Dublin Socialist Club. There he brought out from 1896 to 1903 the first series of his newspaper, *The Workers' Republic,* where he hammered out first principles and the question of Socialism as applied to Ireland. Thence the career continued on the same international plane on which it started. He was an Irishman, and we rightly claim him as ours: but he was born in Edinburgh, and the magnitude and pain of his struggle there gave him every right to Scottish nationality also. He died in Dublin, but some of his greatest work as a labour organiser was in Belfast. Nor may we forget how he became a part of the American labour movement, how he fought and starved there, wrote and organised, met and worked with some of the most remarkable American men and women in the labour movement and was acknowledged by them as equal or superior.[21] I have spoken of him as a major figure in an extremely exciting generation in Irish history, but it must also be stressed that he cannot be seen as Ireland's alone. He was in truth a citizen of the world, and in particular, of the Irish world.

For it is a great error on our part to see Irish history as purely Irish. In the wake of our emigrants, Irish history has become a part of British, American and European history, and Connolly played his role in eastern and western hemispheres in the community of workers the bulk of whom were of Irish birth or ancestry. In one sense he worked on both sides of the Atlantic at once. Desmond Ryan in *Remembering Sion* has captured for us the way in which the fires he had lit in Ireland still smouldered awaiting his return to rekindle them into burning flame. Meanwhile they remembered his teaching:

> One name and one presence pervades the little room: Connolly away in the States. He is the master spirit who has called and held these men together, but somehow they lack his reality and fire. . . . Yet the voice in the darkness who hates the priests and patriots somehow is real, as real as the dank riverside and stinking tenements, the cap-crowned, livid, hopeless, half-fed workers with lined faces and rotting teeth and casts in their eyes, their swarming children and betimes drunken wives, no book worth reading in their sorry homes and little romance save a picture of Parnell or Emmet or a red light before a statue of the Virgin or Christ. What joy or wisdom has the Socialist God over the mantel for them? But the Socialists are right in this too: what change or hope for them when a Green Flag flies over the Castle at the end of the street?[22]

From the experience which Connolly derived from the United States, and the work he did there, came a new dimension to his message on his return. That message was to be one of far more than Irish nationalism, but also far more than Socialism considered without reference to the deepest Irish realities. The important factor for an Irish student of Connolly concerning his work in America, and in Scotland, and its effects on his thought, is that it gave him the sense which so often Ireland could lack, the realisation that the true Irish struggle formed part of a world struggle. He saw that it was as hopeless for the Socialist to preach his philosophy without any reference to its specific area of intended impact, as it was for the nationalist to try to preach doctrines which had no social content and no international sense.

Connolly thought very deeply on the question of internationalism in outlook for the Irish, because time and again in his work among the Irish emigrants in Britain and America he came up against the absence of an international sense on the part of these emigrants. He saw that the emigrant process was an extraordinarily cruel one, tearing up the peasants from the land, driving them across the sea, forcing them to fight their way for survival through some capitalist hell's kitchen. But this process was a very hardening one, which bruised the mind, rigidified it and bred within it a cruelty in order to get ahead. At the same time the process brought with it an increased herd-instinct among the Irish, strengthening Irish parochialism and sense of self-sufficiency. It tended to make the Irish emigrants give themselves wholly unreal airs, see themselves as a people apart, and regard themselves as somehow immune to or above any form of association with other ethnic groups. No man took greater care than Connolly to ensure that as far as he was concerned the Irish would be forced to recognise their international place, and their need for solidarity with all other races. He hit Irish notions of racial superiority at their kernel, the Irish sense of historical uniqueness. 'Perhaps no race on earth', he wrote when editing *The Harp* in New York in 1908,

> has absorbed more heterogeneous elements into itself and at the same time given out more of the best of its blood to the upbuilding of foreign and alien races than the Irish. . . . the Irish, to whom our capitalist politicians are forever preaching an aggressive insularity (as if a man could not love his own without hating his neighbor), can count as cousins and blood brothers practically all the nations of Europe. We have received and we have given the best and the worst. . . . Let no Irishman throw a stone at the foreigner; he may hit his own clansmen. Let no foreigner revile the Irish; he may be vilifying his own stock.[23]

He stressed internationalism above all, seeing as he had done the bitter ethnic warfare in the emigrant ghettoes, warfare he had witnessed from Glasgow to New York, from Boston to Dundee, where Irish Catholic fought Ulster Presbyterian, and both fought Italians and Jews and Negroes and Poles. He relentlessly insisted that his countrymen recognise that their primary role was as members of the working class, in which other emigrant groups had a part to play. And as the above extract shows, he saw and stressed that ethnic division was capitalist-fostered and only to capitalist advantage. He forced his fellow-countrymen to smash the ethnic chains which bound them, and to recognise that in so far as they got involved in stupid ethnocentricity and national conceit, they were destroying themselves as far as any chance of forcing their rights was concerned.

And he most bitterly assailed those persons who tried to cater to Irish national conceit and win cheap popularity by saluting his countrymen as a chosen people or in similarly nonsensical terms. He had a short way with such intellectually dangerous messages:

> We are a great people! Mr Yeats comes all the way from Ireland to tell us in New York that we Irish are a spiritual-minded people, and every Irish saloon keeper in America swells with pride as he reads the modest eulogium, and then passes on the graft to the District Leader, to allow him to break the law and keep open on Sunday.... When W. B. Yeats, son of the gentleman whose remarks elicited the above comment, produced in Ireland a play, 'The Countess Cathleen', which purported to treat of a mythical Irish lady who in a time of famine sold her soul to the Devil in return for food for the starving people—all the spiritual-minded journalists in Ireland were horrified at the suggestion that an Irish woman would do such an act. Yet not one of them could go to or from the newspaper office of an evening without passing scores and sometimes hundreds of Irish girls whom the pressure of want had driven to sell themselves body and soul for a crust of bread and a slum to hide their misery in.[24]

No, Connolly was not prepared to live in some sort of happy Irish club. He was prepared to turn his indignation at Irish self-absorption upon any man—or any group—which chose to foster such delusions. It is of particular interest to note therefore that in the early stages of the rise of the Sinn Féin party Connolly took pains to stress firstly, that it was wise for the Irish to acquire a distinctive Irish sense, to solve their problems in an Irish context, and to study the Irish language if need be since it would give reassurance and increase self-confidence:

> I cannot conceive of a Socialist hesitating in his choice between a policy resulting in . . . self-abasement, and a policy of defiant self-reliance, and confident trust in a people's own power of self-emancipation by a people.[25]

He is thinking there specifically of the suggestion that the Irish should accept the English language as their sole tongue, because it is the language of commerce and of officialdom, as opposed to learning and employing Irish as a spoken tongue. But as for Sinn Féin and its national aspirations such as the 'restoration of the Irish parliament' and a dual monarchy on Austro-Hungarian lines as put forward by Arthur Griffith in *The Resurrection of Hungary*, Connolly is blunt:

> As a cold matter of fact all talk about the 'Restoration of our native Parliament' is misreading history. Ireland never had an Irish Parliament—a Parliament representative of the Irish people. The assembly called by the name of an Irish Parliament was in reality as alien to the Irish people as the Council of the Governor-General of India is alien to the Indian people. And some of the laws passed by our so-called native Parliament against the poor Irish peasantry were absolutely revolting in their ferocity and class vindictiveness. . . . This is not 1782, this is 1908 and every political or

social movement which hopes for success must express itself in terms of present conditions, or on the lines of future developments. . . . during the early stages of the movement in Ireland before the felicitous name of Sinn Féin was coined, the ideas as promulgated got the name of 'the Hungary system'.

I remember one critic declaring that 'the Hungary system was only fit for hungry men'.[26]

In plain language he testified that there was no sense to a self-deluding policy founded on a misreading of history chosen on some inadequate parallel, losing sight of the essential social needs of the people, and failing by its lack of an international sense to see that the worst enemies of Irishmen were only too often other Irishmen.

Time and again Connolly found himself coming up against the Sinn Féin mentality which held that because he was an internationalist he must therefore be untrue to Ireland. He answered it readily:

Internationalism! To some people this is the great bug-a-boo which frightens them off from Socialism. It is international. Therefore they say it is anti-patriotic and ought to be suppressed.

Particularly among the Irish men and women do we find this objection exploited. To the average non-Socialist Irishman the idea of belonging to an international political party is unthinkable, is obnoxious, and he feels that if he did all the roots of his Irish nature would be dug up.

Of course he generally belongs to a church—the Roman Catholic Church—which is the most international institution in existence. That does not occur to him as atrocious, in fact he is rather proud than otherwise, that the church is spread throughout the entire world, that it overlaps the barriers of civilisation, penetrates into the depths of savagedom, and ignores all considerations of race, color or nationality.[27]

It seems to me that Connolly is not here using the example of the Roman Catholic Church as a debating-point only. He is carefully analysing the implications of Catholicism for its believers, and pointing out, as regards the word 'Catholic' itself, how inescapable was a Socialist conclusion for those who accept Catholicism literally as well as metaphorically. He continued, in this passage, to ridicule the mentality of those ethnocentric Irish who failed to apply their alleged Catholic attitudes to Socialism:

It appears that an international Church as a guide to happiness in the next world is a revelation from God, but happiness in this world is an invention of the devil.

An Irish Catholic family in America will listen with bowed heads and reverent hearts whilst an evangelical from an Italian Pope is read in church on Sunday, and on Monday will serve notice upon their landlord that they intend to leave his house because he has permitted some Italians, countrymen of the Pope, to move into the same street.

Irish bricklayers in New York object to working beside Italian bricklayers, but look with religious awe upon an Italian Cardinal.

Irish men in the Democratic party support the acts to exclude the Chinese from this country as unfit to mix among white people, but when the great Li Hung

Chang came to New York and objected to the trouble of walking, Irish members of the New York police force were ordered by their Tammany Chiefs to bow their necks to the yoke of his palanquin and carry the fat Celestial wherever he wanted to go.

It is clear from this passage that Connolly was reminding his fellow-countrymen continuously that anti-internationalism was a capitalist doctrine sown amongst them and alien to their true nature and most deeply-held beliefs; but that capitalism itself, in his view, was far less ready to remain committed to the doctrine than were its poor dupes, the Irish workers, and that whenever expediency dictated it, capitalism would force its dupes to become as internationalist in their behaviour as the maximum profit might require.

Another point to be made from these arguments is that while Connolly made the maximum usage of a common frame of reference with the Irish emigrant audience whom he hoped to influence, he was remorseless in his refusal to butter the Irish up. The most comforting form of nationalism, that which flatters the intended convert by ascribing a natural superiority to his race, was totally abhorrent to him. He was seeking to make converts to Socialism: but he absolutely declined to sugar the pills he administered. As he saw it, capitalism had been fortified, his fellow-countrymen debased and much evil created by the fostering of immigrant tensions, whether through foolish talk or malignant intention. He favoured nationalism in so far as it advanced a desire for the betterment of human dignity, or gave a sense of community, or increased the pride of self-respect among the working class. But if he was to work with nationalism he had to cut out the cancer which was eating it up, the cancer of belief in the inferiority of other ethnic groups. Connolly as a student of British imperialism well knew this cancerous growth within nationalism to be at the heart of the defence of the imperial idea. He saw this cancer in its most malignant form among the Irish emigrants abroad, but he also recognised the early forms of it at home, in the Sinn Féin movement and elsewhere. Connolly was a nationalist: but there can have been few nationalists more aware than he of the distortions and sicknesses from which nationalism, to be justifiable, must be purged.

2

Connolly and Catholicism

> ... *the Catholic Church is theoretically a community in which the clergy are but the officers serving the laity in a common worship and service of God, and ... should the clergy at any time profess or teach doctrines not in conformity with the true teachings of Catholicity it is not only the right, but it is the absolute duty of the laity to refuse such doctrines and to disobey such teaching.*[1]

Connolly's references to the Catholic Church lead us to ask what was his position *vis-à-vis* the Church? In addressing myself to this, I think that first of all I should seek to stress the need for the commentators themselves to take as part of their own outlook something of Connolly's receptivity and readiness to acknowledge common ground. The sectarianism against which Connolly struggled so well during his lifetime, whether in his opposition to sterile forms of nationalism, or in his critiques of rigid, self-righteous Socialist dogmatists such as Daniel De Leon, has been noticeable in much of the comment and observation on him since his death. I don't allude to his obvious enemies: bourgeois nationalists who regard his Socialism as something, at best, to be glossed over, reactionary clericalists who regard him as fundamentally anti-religious and hateful in his message, opponents of the labour movement who sought in his lifetime to destroy him and pressed for his ultimate execution. These men, even the last group, are today represented by the mentality which asserts its readiness to glorify the dead Connolly and is most anxious to hide all trace of the living Connolly. But sectarians do exist among the ranks of Connolly's friends, admirers and disciples, men who in all good faith revere his memory, yet hold that he could not have been both Socialist and Catholic; and hence the Catholics among them deny his Socialism, while the Socialists deny his Catholicism. Their error arises through their basic, but somewhat arid, honesty. Their position makes for an intellectual exclusiveness which in my view Connolly would have been the first to deplore.

I would myself take the view that this effort to argue that the camps of Socialism and Catholicism are mutually exclusive and that Connolly must be thrust into one or the other, arises from a fundamental misunderstanding of both doctrines. I have already suggested that Connolly's Socialism derived its richness from the extent of his range of investigation and from his receptivity to intellectual stimulus, while it remained unshakeable in its firm basis. I would go on to argue that Connolly's Catholicism was also a belief rooted in firm soil but highly receptive to influence from a multitude of sources and enunciated in a fashion which took it far beyond the spirit of his times. It seems to me that Connolly perceived, as few men by his time had done, an essential inter-dependence of Catholicism and Socialism. From this he went on to put forward positive reflections on Catholicism which make him, in my view, one of the best and most enlightened apologists the Catholic Church has seen since the Industrial Revolution. Many commentators have been misled by the utter refusal of Connolly to indulge in mealy-mouthed face-saving so far as the shortcomings of Catholic churchmen and policies were concerned: when he considered something to be wrong, i.e. contrary to justice and truth and hence the spirit of Catholicism, he said so. St Thomas More, another Catholic apologist of the Connolly type, whom Connolly himself quoted and greatly admired, took the same approach: but by Connolly's time a pusillanimity had become fashionable which involved the cowardly belief that the admission of blots on the Catholic record meant giving aid and comfort to the enemies of Catholicism. Connolly was an exception in his readiness triumphantly to acknowledge that wrong had been done, and that redemption could only be achieved by acknowledging the wrong and learning from it. Moreover, I am convinced that in much that Connolly wrote about Catholicism there is the genuine disgust of a true Catholic for the means by which his religion has been debased, dragged into the service of contemptible and evil causes, and re-interpreted in ways that insulted God and man.

This Catholicism of Connolly's has perhaps been missed by many people because Connolly carried out his work in the forum of working-class politics and social conflict: but one cannot deny the force of a theologian merely because he does not use theological terminology, write for an audience of fellow-theologians or publish his arguments in theological journals. 'It seems likely', observed Father Lambert McKenna in his seminal essay, 'that his ideas were far more orthodox than his phrasing of them.'[2] The example McKenna cites is Connolly's comment on another clerical social commentator. Connolly remarks, in the passage quoted by McKenna, that 'the differences' between himself and the Capuchin, Father Lawrence, 'were apparently only differences of definition. The Reverend Lecturer called things by certain names; we would use totally different names, but in essence the things were identical.' It seems probable that today the intellectual heirs of Father Lawrence might find that Connolly's definitions have stood the test of time better than those of his ally, but at all events Connolly had no choice in the matter of definitions. Theology is, in its essence, a science whose definitions embody nuance, philosophical reflection and, above all, the consideration of the concrete in the language of the abstract. Connolly had necessarily to employ language in a wholly different way. The theologian, until he comes into the arena of human affairs in practice as well as in theory, will state his propositions in the form of intellectual exercise. Connolly was speaking to workers, and his words had to possess bite, and fight, and grip. Connolly's work, as I believe he saw it, was God's work, but its language, its definitions and its expression had to be put in terms that his audience would be fired by, and that the conditions he was fighting themselves demanded. But, however important to his work his definitions were, Connolly never lost his sense of priorities. As he wrote in the same passage on Father Lawrence:

We both endorsed the principle embodying the

things whose names we could not agree upon. For that reason we on our part being more anxious for satisfactory results than for correct definitions would not press to contention any of the seeming points of difference.[3]

These remarks throw much light on Connolly's flexibility as a propagandist while underlining his commitment to basic principle; and, as Lambert McKenna said, they also stress his own essential concord with Catholicism; but I feel that they also reveal clearly how strong his conviction was that his work was Father Lawrence's work, and the work that all other priests should be doing.

I suspect that many good Catholics have, in their zeal to include Connolly among the votaries of Catholicism, expended their energies in seeking to make him orthodox by the standards of his day. I think that the boot is on the other foot: Connolly has to be seen as a Catholic who was decidedly progressive by the standards of 1968, and I am quite sure that reflective Catholics will find him fully as progressive, thought-provoking and forceful a critic in the year 2000 as he is now. If non-Catholics will forgive my speaking for a moment in primarily Catholic terms, may I say that we are only ready for him now. We were far, far behind him in 1916. Everything that is now being very fumblingly done in order to give a sense to Catholics of what their Church is all about is, when at its most significant, what Connolly himself was saying.

It was as a Catholic no less than as a Socialist that he expressed his deepest horror at efforts to prostitute the Church in the interest of capitalism. We can, I think, in the following passage trace a direct descent from Christ's words to the money-changers in the Temple:

It is not Socialism but Capitalism that is opposed to religion; Capitalism is social cannibalism, the devouring of man by man, and under capitalism those who have the most of the pious attributes which are required for a truly deeply religious nature are the greatest failure and the heaviest sufferers.

Religion, I hope, is not bound up with a system founded on buying human labor in the cheapest market, and selling its product in the dearest; when the organised Socialist Working Class tramples upon the Capitalist Class it will not be trampling upon a pillar of God's Church but upon a blasphemous defiler of the Sanctuary, it will be rescuing the Faith from the impious vermin who make it noisome to the really religious men and women.[4]

No Socialist who respects the name of Connolly could do less than grant the utter sincerity of that protest. No Catholic who is prepared to think about his religion can deny the force and relevance of it for 1968 as well as for the time when it was written, sixty years ago. Perhaps by today we have come to see that capitalism has indeed subordinated religious sentiment to the naked dictates of crass materialism. The extraordinary increase in the structure of communication since Connolly's day has brought capitalism to justify itself in far more open terms, and far cruder language, as it preaches its ethic to millions. Now we stand in a world whose mass media of press and television are drenched and saturated with expressions of this ethic, with its efforts to create avarice, envy, gluttony, sloth, pride and lust for the sole purpose of increasing markets. With this knowledge, is it too much to expect that we can at last recognise the validity of Connolly's message, and that the Catholic whose forbears feared Connolly as a materialist will see at last that Connolly was in fact the truest defender of spiritual values in a world hell-bent for the materialism which has been achieved in our own day? Connolly, being a disciple of Marx, was charged with materialism in that his thought owed much to the Marxist system of dialectical materialism. I think we now know that there are far worse forms of materialism than the dialectical kind; secondly, we may have learned that intellectual obligation to a system of ideas does not mean being imprisoned in that system—or, in plain language, because Connolly saw that there was much of value in Marx's ideas on man this did not oblige him to assent to Marx's ideas on God, any more than he accepted Marx's views on drink. (Marx was of course the better Irishman here: he enjoyed a drink and Connolly never touched it.) And, thirdly, just as Connolly himself saw that one should not be preoccupied by philosophico-theological terms in putting a case to a working man, so we must realise that we can misinterpret the real value of Marxism by getting bogged down in philosophical labels. Marxism is in fact concerned with what are spiritual questions. Man's right to live is a spiritual question, and we, living after the pontificate of John XXIII, should be ready to recognise as he did that Marxists have been preoccupied by this to a degree that shames many men of so-called spiritual values.

Thomas Bell, a Socialist comrade of Connolly's who was a sceptic in religious matters, has an interesting recollection for us on this point (to which Desmond Ryan initially drew attention):

Connolly . . . never failed, too, in his denunciation of the Church, to make clear he was a Catholic. This was rather disquieting to me . . . I could never understand how it was possible to reconcile this with his profound knowledge of historical materialism. One night, following a meeting in Rutherglen, where the straight question was asked, 'Was he a Catholic?' and the straight reply given, 'Yes', I tackled him on this. 'How is it possible', I asked, 'to reconcile the Catholicism of Rome with the materialist conception of history?' 'Well', he replied, 'it is like this. In Ireland all the Protestants are Orangemen and howling jingoes. If the children go to the Protestant schools they get taught to wave the Union Jack and worship the English king. If they go to the Catholic Church they become rebels. Which would you sooner have?'[5]

In this answer, it seems to me, Connolly revealed a lot of things. Firstly, he showed his humour and what was interlocked with it, his calmness. As we know, he did not see much value in disputing nice points in philosophy, and while he would register the existence of difference on them, he would not let them stand in the way of the positive work that had to be done. If Bell had hoped to lure him into a protracted discussion on the merits of religion and scepticism, he had chosen the wrong man: Connolly knew that nothing was more productive of loss of time and temper and absence of worthwhile practical results than argument about philosophical or religious principles. Constructive exchanges were a different matter, but a discussion such as this would not have been constructive. Moreover Connolly would have known—

no doubt it was as true of his day as it is of ours—that Socialist unity can evaporate overnight in face of an argument on transubstantiation or on what Marx meant by working capital in the surviving fragments of *Das Kapital*, vol. III. Also, Connolly's ready humour made it very easy for him to supply an answer which would be hard for Bell to gainsay and which would forestall any further argument.

Secondly, Connolly's answer was in many ways a very profound one in ways which Catholics should ponder. It was a short-term answer in that it showed a practical advantage of Catholicism which shut Bell up. But on a deeper level it suggested a historical revolutionary mission for Catholicism. Connolly himself, a very detached critic indeed, noted that throughout history the institution of Roman Catholicism normally made terms with any established regime in the end, however critical it might have been of the theory and practice of that regime in its early stages.[6] He went on to argue that the most establishment-minded members of the Catholic world would come to similar terms with Socialism when it should be established. But this sensible analysis would not have prevented him from seeing that Catholicism could and should be a religion of dissent and rebelliousness against the *status quo*, particularly in its application to the peasantry and the working class. I think that his reply to Bell suggested as much, and that the lesson was there for Bell to read if he wished to do so.

Yet we may press Bell's question farther. Connolly was not merely a historian, but one whose sense of the importance of history and of Marxism led him to make some very remarkable applications of Marxist techniques to Irish history. What was his attitude to historical materialism? It seems to me that the answer lies once more in Connolly's vigorous Catholicism. Being a convinced Catholic, he was peculiarly revolted by the notion that God was in some way to be charged with responsibility for the condition of the down-trodden masses. Nothing appalled him more than the efforts which capitalism and its defenders made to justify *laissez-faire* by some sanctimonious and hypocritical appeal to a divine plan: as though God had chosen to contrive the enslavement of the working classes and their exploitation. History, as Connolly saw it, was the record of man's exploitation by man, and all attempts to drag in God as an *alibi* for man's more contemptible actions were blasphemy (the word, let us remember, is his). Connolly was as revolted by the concept of history being God's fault as he was by the notion that the economic circumstances of his day were to be ascribed to God. As I see it, Connolly saw God's place in history as a force which would lead men to hurl themselves against the forces of mammon, and his opponents who gave themselves no greater duty than pitying and donating charity to the poor he denounced as collaborators with mammon. In replying to a clerical critic, he summed up his agenda as one of 'appealing to that individuality, to that national honour, to that heroic spirit in the poor and asking them so to manifest themselves as to rescue their lives from the control of the forces of mammon'.[7] Thus an irony lies at the root of Connolly's view of history and life: he brought back a true concept of man's responsibility for his history, and restored our vision of the goodness of God by refusing to ascribe to God the crimes of man. The character of his thought here is at once a demonstration of his strength as a Socialist and as a Catholic. It also reminds us how his logical and utterly just mind recoiled from the sloppiness and dishonesty of thought which are so prevalent in our day as in his. To take but one example: Connolly demonstrated the degree to which the Irish famine was not, in the common cliché, a 'natural disaster' (i.e. God's fault), but rather a product of some men's crimes and some men's blunderings and some men's refusal to see what steps must be taken to seize control of their destinies.

We can, I think, find one point in Connolly's view of history in which he differs from certain Marxists. The Marxist pattern of successive class struggles can lead to an assumption that men do certain things in the course of these struggles as a result of their class background and class interests, and that these actions are things which must inevitably happen. Connolly was, I think, charitable in allowing for the degree to which economic and social environment could sap a man's perspective, but he was never ready to eliminate the duty of all men to behave with justice and righteousness. He would make allowance for class factors in explaining human behaviour: but he could not admit that this eliminated human responsibility.

Connolly's internationalism was of course as significant a force in his critiques of contemporary Catholicism as in his analysis of the prospects and dangers ahead of Irish nationalism. As we have seen, he noted the symbols of internationalism inherent in Catholicism. But just as Irish nationalism—or any nationalism—could suffer from a sickness whereby in its lack of self-confidence it sought to reassure itself by vilifying other peoples, so the

Catholicism of Connolly's day often revealed its own weaknesses by entirely negative expressions of belief, i.e. by violent attacks on those of other or no religious beliefs not in terms of those beliefs or unbeliefs but simply to rouse solidarity in its own ranks through an appeal to bigotry. The xenophobia of nationalism has been analysed by Professor Higham and others as the essential product of defensiveness, lack of self-assurance and a general fear arising from a repressed belief that it is unable to withstand the impact of alien cultural forces.[8] The same lack of confidence and secret fear of vulnerability led many nationalists to make the wildest claims for the greatness of their nation, to insist on a diet of unctuous, unceasing, totally unrestrained national self-flattery. Irish society at the commencement of the twentieth century contained a myriad of ideologies, as we have seen, and was so much the product of intellectual excitement and cultural ferment that it defies categorisation as either confident or lacking in confidence. But the prophets of fear, with their negative nationalism and xenophobia, were abroad, and there was a danger that they might win a large audience. It was this danger which Connolly saw and combated, both in the much less self-confident nationalism of the emigrant Irish and in Ireland itself. But precisely the same problems affected Catholicism in Connolly's day, and it seems to me that he undertook and discharged the same historical function. Catholicism, also, had its prophets of fear who preached a calculated bigotry born of the belief that Catholics could not withstand the cultural pressures of other doctrines. The same lack of self-confidence brought widespread insistence that Catholics must never admit that any Pope had been a bad man, any Catholic regime had been unjust, or any Papal political decision had been wrong. Among the very finest Catholic writers in the English-speaking world, men such as Chesterton and Belloc, it is all too easy to find evidence of this lack of self-confidence, defensiveness without considering the merits of individual cases, and collapse into bigotry: and these men were great men, with major positive contributions to make. (Chesterton and Belloc themselves, for instance, made some masterly criticisms of the capitalist system and did much to awaken Catholics on social justice.) Now, if at this remove in time we can acknowledge that the crusading zeal of Belloc and Chesterton could embrace religious bigotry (notably virulent hatred of the Jews), and that many of their very good and well-taken defences of Catholicism against the false history of a bigoted Protestant establishment cannot allow us to forget their bad and unsound defences made where honest admissions of wrong were required: then we must also realise that a great mass of Catholic writing and speaking of the day embraced the same bigotries without the good and great qualities. This writing is not generally known to us; it has not withstood the test of time, nor did it deserve to. But it was omnipresent in Connolly's day.[9]

We have to understand this—and in our post-Vatican II era it may not be easy or comfortable to recall such a past—in order to appreciate how far Connolly was in advance of his contemporary fellow-Catholics. In place of the tortuous defences of Catholicism in history he offered a consistently clear and sensible readiness to keep the record straight, to be second to none in his capacity to admit the blots on the Catholic record, and to note where the achievement of Catholicism had been beneficial and worthy of stimulating future action. Again, his Socialism was, as I have indicated, deepened and strengthened by his Catholicism: but the reverse was also true, in the sphere of attitudes to non-Catholics as much as elsewhere. Here is Connolly's famous peroration to *Labour, Nationality and Religion,* a work conceived in the context of a specifically Catholic controversy:

> The day has passed for patching up the capitalist system; it must go. And in the work of abolishing it, the Catholic and the Protestant, the Catholic and the Jew, the Catholic and the Freethinker, the Catholic and the Buddhist, the Catholic and the Mahometan will co-operate together, knowing no rivalry but the rivalry of endeavour toward an end beneficial to all. For, as we have said elsewhere, Socialism is neither Protestant nor Catholic, Christian nor Freethinker, Buddhist, Mahometan nor Jew; it is only *HUMAN*. *We of the Socialist working class realise that as we suffer together we must work together that we may enjoy together.* We reject the firebrand of capitalist warfare and offer you the olive leaf of brotherhood and justice to and for all.[10]

It conveys the gulf between our day and his as does nothing else that this sentiment must have appeared wholly unpalatable to many of his co-religionists. Today we must recognise it as a stirring statement of the priorities. But instead of congratulating ourselves that we live in an ecumenical age, I think we must recognise that it performs for us a critical service also—not merely does it remind us that many men have walked hard and lonely roads to bring us to ecumenism, but it also adjures us to be ecumenists with a powerful, hard sense of solidarity instead of some frothy benevolence which will evaporate at the first gust of bitter wind. And it also stresses that ecumenism will only be welded in the furnace of struggle for true social justice.

If any point in Connolly's life is to be singled out for assessment in connection with his religious attitudes, I think it must be his Belfast years (notably 1911-1913). It was there he witnessed most strikingly the degree to which religious sectarian bitterness divided the working class and bade fair to make it defenceless against the employers and against the magic beat of Carson's drums. In his antagonist, the Home Rule leader and Catholic ghetto boss 'Wee Joe' Devlin, he recognised a major agent in the promulgation of religious sectarianism as well as a force as actively engaged in support of the Catholic petty capitalists as were Carson's friends on the side of the wealthier Protestant capitalists. The two adversaries were symbolically well chosen: against the internationalist Connolly, with his anti-sectarian attitudes in politics and religion, and his unflinching commitment to the destiny of Labour there stood the self-absorbed, embittered opponent of Labour whose mind never thought outside the terms of the political machinery of the Belfast Catholic wards. When Connolly denounced Home Rule as doing nothing to ensure economic liberty for Ireland, he had in mind a vision of his country under the perpetual control of the Joe Devlins who would rule in the interests of their economic masters such as William Martin Murphy. Connolly was out to free Catholicism, as well as to free Ireland, from the rule of the Devlins and

Murphys. And with his remarkable capacity for seeing the realities in individual cases, it is significant that when the nationalist M.P.s at Westminster supported the British war effort in 1914–16, Connolly turned his most bitter assaults on Devlin. Redmond and the bulk of the Irish party had perhaps the excuse that years of preoccupation with Westminster had deHibernicised them, had taken them out of the context of Irish realities altogether. But Joe Devlin, to whom so many of the Belfast Catholics had given their trust, was fully in touch with his constituents, and he knew very well how in exhorting them to join the British forces he was bargaining with lives placed in his trust. Thus it is that for Devlin Connolly reserves the cold fury which is turned on the traitor alone. And the worst taunt he could throw against Redmond and his followers was that they were Devlin's men and the prisoners of the machine he sought to extend to the whole of Ireland. Connolly in the end saw Devlin as little better than the murderer of his own people:

> The present writer cannot ride up the Falls Road in his own motor car, the penny tram has to do him. But thank God, there are no fresh made graves in Flanders or the Dardanelles filled by the mangled corpses of men whom he coaxed or bullied into leaving their homes and families.[11]

Yet with all of his savage indignation, Swiftian in its depth and its zeal to expose cruelty and treachery, his sardonic humour never deserted him. Devlinism had played a terrible part in destroying working-class solidarity in Belfast, and had turned a thriving labour movement in the early years of the century into a faction-ridden nest of religious hatred. Yet Connolly maintained command of his sense of absurdity as he wrote of the poverty of Devlin's Orange opponents and the shamelessness of the ghetto boss himself:

> In the debate in the House of Commons on the M'Cann case, Mr Joseph Devlin, M.P. taunted the Orange bigots with the fact that none of their clergymen had been on the Anti-Sweating platform in the Ulster Hall, Belfast. As a matter of fact, the same was true of the Catholic clergymen. None of them were on that platform either, but the stupid Orange reactionaries could not think of a better answer to Joe than to deny the fact of the sweating. The obvious retort was apparently beyond their capacities.[12]

Joe Devlin, of course, had every reason to discourage attention from being focused on Catholic sweating. But although Connolly believed that Devlin had created a situation in which 'every man who dares to oppose the Redmondite party, or every man within that party who opposes the [Devlinite] A.O.H., must be at all times prepared to take his life in his hands', he could pause to laugh at the absurdities which allowed Devlin to flourish even when he was writing of physical attacks which Devlin's organised mobs had made on himself and his followers.

Whether in debating the heights of political theory, or in analysing the depths of political practice, Connolly never moved far from his sense of humour. An example lies at hand in a much more pleasant context, and the example in this case is one which conveys many lessons.

Connolly's mentor, Karl Marx, produced some of his finest writing in response to opponents whose influence on Socialism he deplored, or sought to modify. Similarly Connolly was led to prepare certain of his most remarkable papers in response to theoretical opponents, but where Marx was writing against other German philosophers Connolly, conscious of the priorities in his Irish or Irish-emigrant context, engaged in debate with other Catholic social theorists. Where Friedrich Engels measured swords with Dühring, Connolly found his Dührings in Father Robert Kane, S.J.,[13] and Father Thomas Finlay, S.J. But, being Connolly, he was insistent on knowing his man, and he found in Father Finlay a protagonist in whom a basis of common understanding existed. It must be stressed that Connolly, in his attitude to Father Finlay, revealed that respect for human dignity which characterised him: he saw, unlike many of his fellow-Socialists, that an opponent could nonetheless understand what Socialism was about, and that Father Finlay did indeed understand it. Many of his Catholic contemporaries would have refused to discuss theoretical (or indeed any) issues with a priest on equal terms: their refusal would probably have been based on the assumption that a priest's cloth made him more than a man, but their attitude in fact made him less than one in that they exempted him from that interchange of discourse which physically separates us from the brute creation. Many of his Socialist contemporaries would have assumed that no priest could possibly have understood what was at issue. Connolly habitually regarded men as worthy of courteous conversation until they showed themselves to be otherwise; and in taking this attitude, he was restoring the rights of priests to be treated as human beings which their enemies, and still more their pious followers, had denied.

In the case of the Reverend Thomas A. Finlay, S.J., subsequently Professor of Economics in University College, Dublin, Connolly was facing a man of intellect and accomplishment who justly enjoyed a high reputation for talents that shone out even in so brilliant a galaxy as that generation afforded. (Ironically, the piety of posterity has chosen to honour Father Finlay by exempting him from that scholarly analysis which his achievements merit, and hence he has yet to receive the place in history which is his due.) Connolly noted that in a lecture on the teachings of Karl Marx given by Father Finlay before the Statistical Society, the priest had given an excellent 'exposition of the evolutionary nature of the socialist doctrine, its historical derivation and materialistic basis'. To Connolly, what was important here was that Father Finlay had shown himself clearly aware of what Socialism was, and this in itself was both an unusual achievement and one of great importance. A crude Socialist would be inclined to ask himself first whether a commentator was for Socialism or not, and only second— if at all—whether he understood it. To Connolly, understanding was the first essential. It was more important than sympathy, for sympathy without understanding was false and insubstantial, and often misleading; whereas understanding without sympathy would either ultimately breed a more co-operative attitude or else create it in others. Connolly was far more confident of good results following from a perceptive analysis of Socialism by Father Finlay, who did not call himself a Socialist, than from any amount of well-meaning nonsensical talk from well-intentioned ignoramuses who proclaimed their Socialism in every sentence.

Connolly's insistence on realistic understanding as the first essential is in itself part and parcel of his own receptivity of mind. He would gladly learn from an opponent if an opponent knew what he was talking about. Moreover, he always had done. We must remember in our efforts to understand Connolly that we have to make ourselves aware not only of what his thought was, but of how he built it up. He put such store on the importance of knowledge, because knowledge had been for him part of the hard struggle that was his life. As we know, the effort for material survival for himself and his family was a cruel and exhausting one for Connolly; but continually alongside it was his equally hard struggle to build up his mental storehouse of fact and theory. The acquisition of knowledge involved greater physical difficulty for him, and greater faith in the need for it, than anything which most of us are likely to have experienced. In his day there was nothing like the extent and variety of communications media which we know today. He drove himself to the pursuit of knowledge with an incessant hunger, and he did so with lack of any comprehensive guide for the assimilation of knowledge and with few systematic pointers for the facts he sought. Such a point as this may seem obvious enough when we think of it, but in our communications-glutted society, are we likely to think of it?

Connolly's faith in the need for true understanding kept him going in the struggle to acquire it through countless frustrations and setbacks. We know how omnivorously he read, and how deeply he cherished such books as he had managed to acquire. We know how purposefully he set himself to the mastery of economics, history and several foreign languages. Italian, for example, he could speak so well as to be accepted by Italians as one of themselves.[14] Yet while we know these things, we can easily lose sight of the idealism which drove him to acquire them despite all the terrible obstacles in the way of doing so. Connolly's struggle for the acquisition of knowledge, and the idealism which drove him to it, are at once a part and a mirror of the wider struggle and wider idealism which characterised his whole life. The knowledge he won was in truth his pearl of great price.

The process of obtaining knowledge dictated certain mental attitudes in him of the kind we have noted. It might have been thought that with the squalor and hardship which formed the economic background to his own life, he of all people had most justification for a Socialism derived from emotional reactions, yet of all people he was the most insistent that emotional response did not begin to fulfil the needs of a Socialist. Hence his enthusiasm for Father Finlay's speech on Karl Marx: to understand Socialism was, for Connolly, to have fought half the battle towards its acceptance. We mistake Connolly if we see him as a crusader against opponents for purely theoretical ends; Connolly engaged in controversy, not to parade his own considerable talents as a controversialist, but to bring his audience nearer truth, whether by hailing understanding or by denouncing ignorance. The battle against ignorance is the keynote of his exposition of Socialism. At the centre of his criticism of the apologists for capitalism lies the charge of intellectual sluggishness and superficiality.

As Desmond Greaves has shown in his masterly biography,[15] Connolly had initially derived his own Socialism in part from study of those who had opposed but shown some understanding of it. As a teacher, he sought to help others discover wisdom by the means he himself had done so. Invariably with him one has the sense that he turned to each new book or paper, not with the question, 'Does this work meet my requirements?', but 'What can I derive from this?' Hence he was able to make the most of the intellectual currents that were aflow in so many directions among his remarkable contemporaries. Hence also we have a clue to the apparent paradoxes of Connolly's being a devoutly spiritual materialist, a Marxist Catholic, and a nationalist internationalist.

Such, then, were the background and basis for Connolly's appreciation of Father Finlay. In addition, Father Finlay's own work in the co-operative movement raised important economic questions and offered the means of enlightening discussion in a field of considerable practical activity. Connolly therefore particularly welcomed any opportunity of commenting on remarks by Finlay, and stressed that any arguments from him both carried weight and deserved serious study. (It is worth underlining this point: Connolly, as a publicist in Ireland, was ready to reply to the comments of any priest whose criticism of Socialism was likely to be of influence, but he drew a sharp distinction between controversy where the object of his reply was of intellectual value in itself, as was normally the case with Father Finlay, and controversy where it was not. The status of priests in Ireland necessitated particular attention to their comments on Socialism: but Connolly paid Finlay the tribute of acknowledging that his intellectual stature won a distinction for his arguments which they held irrespective of the clerical origin of their enunciator.)

In 1899, however, Father Finlay read a paper on 'Co-operation' before the fourth general meeting of the 'Maynooth union' (Connolly's term). In this paper, Finlay suggested that Socialism had much in common with slavery, and, moreover, had 'broken down wherever it has been tried'. Connolly's reply was a charming appeal from Philip drunk to Philip sober. He began by expertly indicating how much Father Finlay's own previous comments on Socialism went to disprove the content of his present remarks. But he went on to make a peculiarly Catholic point with reference to the alleged failure of Socialism wherever attempted:

> The statement was crudely false, mischievous, and misleading, and Father Finlay would not risk his reputation by repeating it before any audience of scientists in the world. That he thought it quite safe to make such an utterance at Maynooth is an interesting indication of the low estimate in which he held the intellectual grasp of his hearers on the thought of their generation. Socialism has not 'broken down wherever it has been tried', because, being the fruit of an historical evolution yet to be completed, *it has never been tried*.[16]

The last statement he based on Father Finlay's own previous analyses, but what concerns us here is the naughty and very perceptive crack about Finlay's attitude to the Maynooth audience. Passing over the question of the attitudes of regular and secular clergy to one another, the more fundamental point remains that Finlay probably doubted whether his Maynooth audience was intellectually capable of accepting the progressive arguments he was normally accustomed to put forward; and he found it expedient to cater to some degree to prevailing prejudices in that quarter in order to bring it a little way with him. Connolly, on the other hand, is still demanding equal rights for priests: Father Finlay, in his view, has a duty to educate Maynooth as great as the duty he normally discharged so well, that of educating the general public.

It is perhaps worth pausing here a moment in order to take up the question of anti-clericalism. In his criticisms of Father Finlay, and in his much more severe onslaughts on less perceptive and enlightened priests, Connolly must be seen as neither pro- nor anti-clerical. His mind was far too serious to be imprisoned in either mould. What is to be found in the Finlay controversy is a civilised exchange between minds of great calibre; and if, in the process, the occasion justly arises to pull Father Finlay's leg, Connolly pulls Father Finlay's leg. The ease with which Connolly, here as always, can appreciate the humour of the situation is in itself an illustration of his objectivity in this theatre. Humour is always the first casualty where either pro-clericalism or anti-clericalism is involved. (Wit, of course, is not, but wit lacks the intellectual sympathy with the situation, the capacity to stand apart, and the ability to laugh at oneself as at others which humour contains.)

Connolly in this was a man of his generation. It was of

course true that the Irish, and still more the Irish-emigrant, communities crawled with the exploitation of religion in the interest of capitalism, as we have noted; and Connolly himself had plenty of experience of arid anti-clericals who had long substituted venom for intellect.[17] But the mass of speakers and writers from whom his generation has won its great name was I think as far removed as he was from crude pro- or anti-clericalist attitudes, and its survivors looked on the bitterness of a later generation with a fastidious distaste and consciousness of the cul-de-sac into which such debates brought intellectual enquiry. The perspective of more recent times may have caused us to lose sight of that mentality. Yet we have had reminders of the realities. For example, when I was a boy it was a commonplace observation that James Joyce was a very anti-clerical, and indeed anti-Catholic, writer. But in recent years we have become acquainted with the writings of his brother Stanislaus Joyce, and in the perspective of their attitudes it has become evident that Stan, and not James, was the anti-Catholic. James was of Connolly's generation; Stan was much younger, in age and still more in his discovery of new mental horizons. We have tended, it seems to me, to confuse the frightened, silent men of the twenties and thirties and the stultifying anti-clericalism of breakaway intellectuals in the same period with a much freer, more thoughtful, more intelligent and more enquiring attitude in the first decades of the century. Few of Connolly's contemporaries brought their detachment into historical writing to the degree that he did, but the best of them resembled him in attitude in this regard. The generation was one where ideals were put forward, considered, accepted and rejected for their own sake rather than for reasons of external pressure, positive or negative. And I think it also resembled him in many cases in its capacity for laughter; it was less easy to find recourse to laughter after the Civil War.[18]

As we have noted, these were also the days of the William Martin Murphys and Wee Joe Devlins and their literary hacks, but Connolly and his leading intellectual contemporaries had the sense to know that in fighting your enemy you do not make the mistake of becoming his mirror image, either by seeking to outbid him in pro-clericalism or by retreating into a correspondingly rigid anti-clericalism. Connolly's own position as a member of the Catholic Church was to take the stand that it is extremely foolish to see its hierarchy and ordained clergy as possessing some special status and exempt from the analysis we give to one another's statements. He did allow for the fact that their public role sometimes gave their statements a special character, but reminded his audience that this public role and its implications could weaken rather than strengthen the force of their argument. On the Holy See's relations with *de facto* regimes which he personally felt should be condemned and repudiated by the workers, he declared:

> ... the Holy See must always acknowledge the *de facto* Government in any country without examining or deciding the question of its rightful title. But the considerations which compel the Holy See, as such, to recognise the *de facto* government and the *de facto* social order are not binding upon individual Catholics, and we, therefore, retain to the full all our rights and

prerogatives as citizens and workers for social betterment, without abating necessarily one jot of our Catholicity.

As individual Catholics, we claim it as our right, nay, as our duty, to refuse allegiance to any power or social system whose authority to rule over us we believe to be grounded upon injustice.[19]

Now, this analysis of course owes something to Daniel O'Connell, however much Connolly might criticise his work elsewhere: another indication of his receptivity. It is also remarkable for its retention of perspective in a context where a later generation assumed it had to choose between Catholicism and Socialism, to the injury both of itself and of the doctrines in question. What Connolly reveals here as elsewhere is an outstanding capacity to judge issues totally without reference to his own ego, where the more self-absorbed dogmatists of a later generation were unable to follow his example.

It is difficult for us to realise that the reflections on social conflict by Connolly which we read today were conceived, for the most part, in the vortex of ferocious controversy. The peace, the confidence, the quietness and calm which pervade the man as he wields his controversial pen make it hard for us to see the incredibly emotive character of the public arena in which he played his part. He wrote with a pungent, argumentative and sometimes highly emotive style: but he was so totally in control of his material, so utterly at peace in his own mind, and so quietly detached in his analyses, that he seems worlds away from later generations who assumed the flamboyant gesture was far preferable to logic and tranquillity of mind. It was his tranquillity which made him as remarkable a man of action as of thought and would enable him to face so stoically the incredible crises of the 1916 period in which even the ever-resourceful and subtle Mac Diarmada was shaken from his normal imperturbability. We find this self-confidence and calm of Connolly's attested to again and again by those who knew him. To be the recipient of a clerical attack is a phenomenon capable of throwing any Irishman (of any denomination) off balance: Connolly was as cool as ice in response to such attack whether literary or oral. His daughter Nora has recalled:

> He came to Mass with me and the priest began to attack without naming him, about something, I forget now it is so long ago. It was something that he was concerned with, and everybody around about knew it was Connolly and you could feel the heads turning around and turning around, from each side, you know, and I put out my hand and said, 'come on, get up and don't stay listening to this' and he just put his hand and sat me down and he said, 'you sit down, you sit down,' he said. 'Let him have his say, we want our say too.'[20]

Connolly's tranquillity and laughter, like Connolly's work and thought, were the product of hardship, and his greatness lay in his retention and increase of these qualities. An instance of this is at hand from his American experience. As we have seen, his work in America involved attacking the susceptibilities and sacred cows of the Irish minority in the United States, yet he was at the same time seeking to learn from them and to teach them, to interest them in his work and to evangelise them. His platform was for the most part his little paper, *The Harp*, whose principle and pungency drove away the readership it desperately needed to survive, and such an apparent dilemma could well have sent another man to pieces. Elizabeth Gurley Flynn, the great American Communist leader, has left us a moving account of his seemingly hopeless efforts to sell the paper to an indifferent Irish-American community.[21] But in the very first issue, Connolly conveyed the reality and the sources of that humour and peace of mind which would sustain him now and in the future:

> ... the writer of these first columns of our paper will ever attune the strains of his harp to the music of the worldwide struggle between the oppressor and the oppressed.
>
> And that struggle has its humorous aspects as well as its tragic. A grave demeanor does not always betoken a serious purpose, and a man offering up his life in martyrdom for a principle may yet march to the scaffold with a joke upon his lips.
>
> Sir Thomas More, scholar and philosopher, executed by Henry VIII of England for refusing to admit the supremacy of that libertine king on religious matters, as he laid his head on the headsman's block asked leave to brush his long-flowing beard out of the way of the executioner's axe. 'For', he said, 'my beard at least has committed no treason' ... let us laugh while we may, though there be bitterness in our laughter; let us laugh while we may, for capitalism has tears enough in store for all of us.[22]

The citation of Sir Thomas More in that passage is, it seems to me, chosen in no idle or casual spirit, but is rather an expression—at the very commencement of what Connolly took to be a critical venture, this editorship of his American journal—of one of the roots of his faith. Connolly stands in the tradition of Thomas More, and sought consciously to do so, in tranquillity and laughter as well as in devotion to principle. He was ultimately to stand in More's tradition in his readiness to accept martyrdom without any desire to thrust himself into martyrdom. He followed More in his insistence on standing by his ideals against the establishment of his day, as More stood by his ideals against the Tudor establishment. And he followed More in recognising, as a Catholic, that zeal for salvation in the next life made it even more incumbent on oneself to fight and write for social justice for others in this one.

Connolly sought to walk in More's footsteps, yet he was himself far too genuine and realistic—and indeed self-effacing—to turn his respect for such an example into a posturing imitation after the manner of some repressed actor. It was More's qualities he strove for, not some mental self-delusion that he was himself another More. Such affectation was totally alien to him. And because nothing could be less contrived than Connolly, one may, I think, say truly that the parallels between the last prison leave-taking of St Thomas More and his wife and daughter, and James Connolly and his, are extraordinary. Both in what was said, and in what neither man could weaken himself by saying, it seems indisputable that to the very end Connolly proved the true successor of More.[23]

APPENDIX TO CHAPTER 2

A note on Catholic Marxism in Connolly's era

Some important work is being done at the present time to suggest the existence of common frontiers between Christianity, specifically Roman Catholic Christianity, and Marxism; the enterprises in question have shown a praiseworthy ambition in concept, if not always a felicity of realisation. But the criticism can be made that here, as elsewhere, the 'New Left' is not always as conscious as it might be that it has had remarkable predecessors. This is a problem less evident in historically-conscious Ireland, where Connolly's memory and writings continue to hold sway among the newest of the 'New Left', than is the case elsewhere. Connolly himself, conscious as he was that many of his ideas were frighteningly new to his Irish audience, was very ready to cite significant antecedents to his own mission. His citation of progressive thought in standard Irish nationalist evangelists is well known; but of even greater importance is his detailed discussion of forgotten Irish precursors of Marx, such as William Thompson, and the makers of the Ralahine experiment, whom he takes under review in Chapters X and XI of *Labour in Irish History*.[24]

Where Ireland in general has less reason to congratulate itself is in knowledge of European antecedents to efforts of this and allied kinds. Connolly's generation and Connolly himself were much better acquainted with the less fashionable forms of cosmopolitan culture than we are—independence, in Ireland, immeasurably increased introversion—but I know of no evidence recording awareness on Connolly's part of the major clerical exponent of Marxist relevance for Christians who was writing in his day. Nevertheless the work of Wilhelm Hohoff deserves notice here as a reminder that Connolly was by no means alone in his efforts to bring together two faiths, Catholicism and Marxism, which are vulgarly taken to be mutually exclusive.

Wilhelm Hohoff would appear to have passed his life entirely in the Prussian province Westphalia, being born in 1848 in the little town of Medebach and dying in 1923 in the cathedral town of Paderborn where he lived for much of his career. He was ordained priest in 1871 and became parish priest of Petershagen, an even smaller town than his birthplace. Hohoff appears to have been driven by a desire to reconcile religion and Socialism; indeed, the word 'reconcile' hardly conveys the spirit of his vigorous asseveration that Catholicism and Socialism mutually support one another. Inevitably, this earned him attacks from both camps, such as Connolly also experienced. Much as Daniel De Leon assailed Connolly's championship of the inviolability of the family, Bebel wrote his *Christianity and Socialism* (1892) as a direct attack on Hohoff. Like Connolly also, Hohoff met with very few adherents, but attracted extensive criticism from sympathetic and hostile Catholic writers, of whom Bishop Ketteler and the historian Jannsen, who at least granted him a kindly hearing, approximate to the position of

Father Finlay in Connolly's case. The famous American priest, Father John A. Ryan, opposed Hohoff's main case, but derived much from his reasoning including strong condemnation of interest on capital. In this, John Ryan's role is comparable to that of Lambert McKenna *vis-à-vis* Connolly, and it is to be regretted that little was done by Catholic writers in America to follow up Ryan's conclusions, or in Ireland, to follow McKenna's. To say this is not to deny that the conservative approach of both Ryan and McKenna was more in keeping with their day than ours; the present generation should confront Connolly—and Hohoff—in their own terms.[25]

Connolly was writing for workers, and was a worker; hence his approach was never particularly theological. Hohoff's work was essentially theoretical and highly theological in orientation. His writings include *Protestantism and Socialism* (1881, second edition 1883), *The Revolution since the Sixteenth Century* (1887), *Ethics of Aristotle and Thomas Aquinas* (1893), *Warenwert and Capital Profit* (1902), *The Meaning of the Marxist Critique of Capitalism* (1908), and *Apology of Christianity* (1909). He does not seem to have attracted translators. His books had some small circulation outside Germany, one or two making their way to French libraries, and rather more to British and American. *The Meaning of the Marxist Critique of Capitalism* particularly interested John Ryan, but its circulation seems to have been limited to Germany and the U.S.A. Ryan summarised its propositions as follows:

1. The Church has never admitted the justice of interest whether on money or on capital, but has merely

tolerated the institution, just as under the Old Dispensation God tolerated divorce and polygamy.

2. She has always denied the productivity both of money and of capital, holding that the only true cause or producer of value is labor.

3. Her teaching concerning the functions and claims of capital and labor is the same as that of Karl Marx.

4. The Marxian theory of value, especially of surplus value, is the true explanation of this fundamental relation.[26]

Interestingly, Hohoff did not subscribe to the Marxist assumption of the ultimate withering-away of the state; nor does Connolly, concerned as he was with immediate questions, appear to have stressed it greatly. Yet it might be felt that so essentially apocalyptic an argument does produce its logical merits for the Christian. The perfectibility of mankind seems as much short of realisation as the withering-away of the state, and yet no Christian is entitled to relax his efforts and hopes for the former, and no Marxist would be advised to lose sight of the latter. Connolly, in his interest in early primitive Irish social organisation—which he viewed with far too benign an attitude—may offer a shadow of involvement in the question, but Hohoff explicitly rejected the doctrine. Were future commentators to examine it, they might well find a synonymous character between human perfection and the state's withering-away.[27]

Where Hohoff and Connolly differed most clearly in their approaches to Catholicism and Marxism, was that Hohoff was concerned with the precept, and Connolly maintained that the precept had to be taken in conjunction with what happened in practice. He would have been interested in Hohoff's conclusions, as he was always interested in evidence that his Catholic fellow-workers had no grounds for theoretical opposition to Socialism, but he would certainly have subscribed to Ryan's view that the Church 'has indeed permitted and authorised (not merely "tolerated") . . . and herself accepted interest on capital; but this does not prove that the practice is directly justified by the principles of strict, or individual, justice'. This is precisely Connolly's approach to such questions. Ryan, no less than Connolly, found himself sharply criticising the views of Irish theologians, in this case the Rev. T. Slater, S.J. and 'my friend, Dr Harty of Maynooth'. Slater asserted:

> By the law of nature, by the very nature of the right of property, whatever a thing produces belongs to the rightful owner of that thing. When the produce is due partly to the natural or artificial fertility of the property, and partly to human labour, both the owner of the property and the labourer have rights in the produce.

And Ryan replied:
> Like charity, the 'law of nature' has for many centuries covered a multitude of sins, intellectual and polemical sins, indeed, but none the less demoralising on that account. The 'natural law', and *res fructificat domino,* are valid within their own sphere, but they too frequently function as substitutes for objective analysis.
>
> . . . The right of private property exists because the institution of private property is essential to individual, as well as to social, welfare; but who can prove that

the receipt of interest on capital is essential to individual welfare, and therefore included in the right of ownership?

After which he went on to note Harty's 'extreme' assertion of the argument against him, 'that the capitalist's right to some interest on his capital is superior to the labourer's right to the minimum wage that will suffice for decent living', a view he simply stated in its nudity as, impliedly, self-condemned. 'Contemporary Catholic writers', observed Ryan, 'are so preoccupied refuting Socialism and defending the present order, that they go to the opposite extreme, understating the amount of truth in the claims of the Socialists, and overstating the rights of property and the advantages of the present system. They forget that the Catholic teaching on wealth and property is, as Abbot Gasquet has said, collectivistic rather than individualistic.'[28]

Ryan's views placed him rather in the school of Hilaire Belloc, G. K. Chesterton and the Distributists than in that of Connolly. But the formidable anti-capitalist logic he brought to his enunciation had much in common with Connolly, while the opponents he directed his shafts against were the same in fact, if not in name, as those whom Connolly was forced to refute. Connolly would not have been sorry to acknowledge Ryan's remarks on the use of natural law as an alibi. Connolly's defences of Socialism against Father Kane and Father MacErlean were demanded by their assertions based on the same premises as those of Dr Harty and Father Slater which drew the ire of Ryan.

It is by no means impossible that Connolly was familiar

with John Ryan's work. The American priest was a distant relative of the labour journalist and editor of the *Irish Peasant* W. P. Ryan, and hence of his son, Connolly's first biographer Desmond Ryan. Connolly knew the Ryans, particularly the father, and John Ryan visited his Irish relatives. But whether a connection can be proved or no, it is evident that Connolly shared with Ryan a conviction that Catholicism must not be sold out to capitalism, while the case of Hohoff reminds us that the climate of the times was productive of other lonely pioneers working on similar lines to himself. A point of difference lies in the fact that Hohoff and Ryan, as priests, had no choice but to explore their urgings for social radicalism in a theological context; Connolly wrote about Catholicism because his area of evangelism was one where Catholicism was the religion of the bulk of the people. Had he escaped altogether from the world of the Irish, and played his part in some non-Catholic environment, he would not have posed and answered his questions in a Catholic framework as Ryan and Hohoff would have done, wherever they were. This is not to say that Connolly would have ceased to be a Catholic were he resident outside a Catholic *milieu*, but that his religion would have become part of his private, spiritual, and hence unknown life instead of having to be dragged into the market-place of controversy as, in Ireland, it had to be.

3

The Problem of the Easter Week Rising

*If these men must die, would it not be better to die in their
own country fighting for freedom for their class, and for the
abolition of war, than to go forth to strange countries
and die slaughtering and slaughtered by their brothers that
tyrants and profiteers might live?*[1]

Where would Connolly stand if he were alive today? He would stand where he always stood, against exploitation of man by man, against sectarianism and bigotry, against small-mindedness and baseless self-congratulation. He would acknowledge the cause of those who today struggle against social injustice and cruelty, as his cause. He would stand by those who struggle not only on behalf of Socialism in his own country but against injustice anywhere in the world. He would be the comrade of those men who, whether priest or atheist, Irish or foreigner, Belfast or Dublin, follow the same ideals which he followed; and he would oppose the materialism of our age as remorselessly as he opposed the materialism of his own. He would be as conscious of the dangers of nationalism and the wrongs it can seek to conceal now as he was then:

> We mean to be free, and in every enemy of tyranny we recognise a brother, whatever his birthplace;

—and in recognition of this doctrine of Connolly's, integral as it is to his thought, the Irish Congress of Trade Unions has placed a very beautiful and inspiring plaque in its building, Congress House in Raglan Road, Dublin, bearing these words. I would wish to compliment Congress on this most fittingly artistic and functional method of honouring Connolly, who of all men would have valued a tribute whose nature was to immortalise the essence of a belief he held so strongly. But a plaque cannot contain more than a few words, or it loses its emotional impact and artistic quality, and neither Connolly nor those who honour him would wish us to forget the lines which follow that quotation:

> in every enemy of freedom we also recognise our enemy, though he were as Irish as ourselves.

It is very right that we should bear in mind now at the centenary of Connolly's birth that Connolly's ideals live both in his writings and in the hearts and minds of men and women who bring them into action today. It is right that we should recall the force of his insistence that Ireland should not and could not concentrate on her own struggle only, but that attention must be paid, as he paid it, to the struggle against oppression in India[2] and elsewhere. It is right that we think of the way in which he sought to bring Irish exiles in America and Scotland to a sense of their obligation to take part in the working-class struggle in their new countries as well as maintaining active interest and sympathy for their comrades remaining in Ireland. This must be our legacy from him. In every enemy of freedom we have to recognise our enemy, without prejudice to national considerations; and in defence of freedom we, in Connolly's name, have to take our stand. By doing so we acknowledge that he whose birth we celebrate himself brought into the world ideas and attitudes we will not let die; by refusing to do so we place ourselves on the same plane as those who demanded and those who ordered his death, for the failure to take up Connolly's banner is in itself a tacit declaration that he is better dead—gloriously dead, of course, but dead none the less.

It was not an easy death to die, this death of Connolly's which so many are anxious to employ as justification for burying his ideas as well as his bones. I do not allude only to the incredible pain of his wound, or to the final impregnation of his exhausted body by excruciating pain at every point in the physical system. The decision to take up arms in 1916 was in itself a decision of pain, and Connolly's wisdom, remarkable as it was, necessarily included the wisdom of sorrow, the foreknowledge that his acts would be misinterpreted and reviled. He, who had so often raised his voice on behalf of the voiceless masses, would now be unable to raise that voice on his own behalf and in explanation of a decision which many men of goodwill would be unable to understand on their own. 'They will never understand why I am here', he told his daughter Nora in prison after the rising, as they spoke of the Socialist newspapers. 'They will all forget I am an Irishman.'[3]

It was not only foreign Socialists who would not understand his action. To the Irishman who thinks of

Connolly primarily as a nationalist, and finds his intellectual problems only in grasping Connolly's Socialism, it may be surprising to learn that others are faced with an equally severe set of problems in accepting him as a nationalist. As Desmond Ryan has put it, 'Connolly was a man who belonged to, and worked in two worlds: the world of international socialism and the world of militant nationalism',[4] but there were some of his closest contemporaries who never recognised this and who went to their graves regarding his final actions as a tragic deviation from his life's work. Those who scrutinise Connolly's writings throughout his life can prove that such men were mistaken: all of the leading scholars on Connolly, from Lambert McKenna to Desmond Greaves, are in agreement on the deep roots of his nationalism, and the degree to which nationalist thought and attitudes affected him throughout the course of his twenty years of literary activity. Nevertheless we must recognise that Connolly took an extraordinarily difficult step in identifying himself with an activist nationalist movement, and just as he criticised Arthur Griffith and his followers for their absence of radical social thought and their exclusivism, so he himself would later be criticised by the embittered Seán O'Casey for having mixed himself up with a nationalist revolt.[5]

Why did he do so? It is not, perhaps, a question which Irishmen would naturally ask in this context, and yet the power and brilliance of O'Casey's writing alone give the question an urgency from which we cannot escape. My own comments earlier in this lecture also prompt a logical query along these lines: if we acknowledge Connolly's receptivity, his retention of principle but insistence on the need for readiness to profit by the possibilities of a situation, and his breadth of awareness of the value of widely differing men and movements, how do we account for his apparently unflinching journey toward insurrection? He knew very well that this course closed option after option to him. Viewed from today, the 1916 Rising seems an incredible gamble on which to risk the sacrifice of all that he had gained. His hopes for Belfast working-class solidarity and success, the status that had been won for the Irish labour movement, the links that had been forged with Socialism elsewhere, his own formidable position as an intellectual and moral force—all were hazarded. His grief in his last days at Belfast's failure to participate in the Rising reminds us how dear to him his hopes for Belfast had been.

In the narrow sense, we have to realise that to Connolly, as to countless other Socialists, the nature and extent of the war which broke out in 1914 transformed the situation utterly. 'And now like the proverbial bolt from the blue, war is upon us', he wrote, 'and war between the most important, because the most socialist, nations of the earth. And we are helpless!'[6] The next two years proved indeed how helpless international Socialism seemed to be, and the British shelving of the Irish question must have seemed but one of the countless changes this war would ruthlessly enforce. Connolly, who possessed gifts of great foresight in times of storm as in those of calm, recognised that the world could never be the same again after the war; as Mr Donal Nevin has put it, in his last two years on earth Connolly saw 'the holocaust of the hopes of his generation'.[7] He had of course only indications of what ultimate changes there would be, but he seems to have been convinced that capitalism would enter on a much more repressive phase—unless in some way it could be halted by something taking place in the cauldron of change itself. He told his followers that the war offered a chance of success, but there he spoke more as propagandist than as teacher. To get his real meaning, we have to look at the obverse of the coin, at the implication that revolutionary action in war offered the only chance of success. To the internationalist that Connolly was, the war must have been infinitely more hideous and loathsome, and far more criminal, than it was to any other of the Easter leaders; and an evil tree would bear evil fruit. The only way, his urgency suggests, that remained to him was to match force with counterforce and ensure that the inevitable changes would weaken and not strengthen capitalism.

It is this conviction, I think, which transformed his thought from an exploitation of favourable currents of ideology and action into a desperately anxious drive toward insurrection. If this is correct, Connolly would have held that the first shots in the Easter Rising were in fact fired in August, 1914, and that he was forced to risk his life's work or helplessly witness its utter destruction. Even for the most receptive man, intellectual interplay must have an end, and a conclusion must be drawn at a time of crisis. Connolly had never hesitated to draw his conclusions, and he did not hesitate in drawing this one. Marxism as ever sharpened his logic and strengthened the force of his analysis, but I am less ready to admit that Connolly was simply playing it by the book than Dr David Thornley—if I interpret him correctly—appears to be.[8] It was Connolly's strength that his use of

Marxism was invariably on the level of employing it as a form of practical clarification, and not of seeking to fit his analysis of the contemporary world into a preconceived Marxist framework. As I suggested earlier, Karl Marx was Connolly's stimulant and teacher, not his intellectual jail-warder. The practical character of Connolly's use of Marxism was once more evident as soon as he had taken the decision to embark on a rising. His writings on revolutionary warfare are a highly impressive series of reflections on historical events possessing lessons which future Dublin insurgents would do well to ponder. In his thoughtful introduction to the first reprinting (1968) of these articles, which originally appeared in 1915, Mr Michael O'Riordan reminds us that Connolly 'approached revolutionary war not as a romantic; he was the least "militaristic" of the 1916 leaders but he saw it as a serious business, subscribing to Engels' dictum that "fighting is to war what cash payment is to trade" '.[9]

Socialism therefore dictated that Connolly would appeal to arms; but nationalism was responsible for his doing so in a specifically Irish context, in alliance with men whose priorities were nationalist rather than Socialist. We must take a larger view to account for Connolly's acceptance of this form of insurrection—an ideological coalition of insurgents as opposed to a small group of revolutionary Socialists pure and simple. Ironically enough, although the Rising necessarily weakened Connolly's effectiveness in the larger ideological breeding-ground in which he had been operating, the idea of a revolutionary coalition was, after all, very much in keeping with his practice of intellectual activity in a wide arena of differing outlooks. Revolutionary activity closed the door to future Socialist evangelisation; yet the form of activity he employed was wholly in keeping with his lifelong methods of evangelisation. As usual, he was increasing the understanding of others by common activity on the widest possible basis. After all, before the war, he had been working with nationalists and interesting them in Socialism by this principle of action on what common basis of agreement there was. Even if Connolly had not strong emotional ties to nationalism in any case, he would have had much reason to look carefully at it, realising as he did that to interest other men in your ideas you have to take stock of theirs. As matters stood, he was prepared to be as good a nationalist as any of them, provided he did not thereby abate one jot of his internationalism. His interest in other men made such a process easier in any case, and he could well make the most of the wide extent of common ground that he actually had with many nationalists. By the time war broke out, Connolly had had a long experience of evangelising nationalists, having, as he had, worked with Plunkett, thrown social ideas into the mind of Pearse, fired AE with enthusiasm, and persuaded the young Maud Gonne to address his meetings and publish his articles, and come along on his marches, dragging poor Willie Yeats after her.

As I stated in the early part of this lecture, Connolly's Dublin was one of incredible intellectual excitement, but also of intellectual interplay, and necessarily so. The minds of that day did not possess their souls in silence and enunciate their private philosophies to themselves without any communication whatsoever. They talked, and argued, and wrote, and acted, alongside each other, against each other, for each other. Intellectual interplay might not be verbal or literary or even dramatic: it could be in the business of some physical activity or in the organisation of a committee or a demonstration. As a result of this interplay Socialists and nationalists came to talk to each other more and more. Sometimes the debate between Connolly and one nationalist might lead to serious soul-searching by another nationalist, as happened when Arthur Griffith attacked the labour movement as a result of which Eamonn Ceannt raised strong criticisms of Griffith. Necessarily both Socialists and nationalists, as they found more and more common ground, were obliged to make certain compromises. To this Connolly was no exception.

The compromise for Connolly was not, of course, that he took part in the Rising of 1916. The compromise was, those with whom he went into it. Several of the insurgent leaders were, as we have noted, strongly under Connolly's influence. Plunkett's case we have examined; Pearse was moving so strongly in Connolly's direction, and was in addition drawing such radical social conclusions from his Gaelic studies, that the Russian Marxist scholar V. Kolpakov has recently been led by his researches to suggest that by 1916 Pearse had arrived at a primitive, but none the less noteworthy, social revolutionary position; Ceannt was prepared to defend Connolly against attack, while not being notably significant in positive contribution to Socialist thought; and other members of the Irish Volunteers at least represented suitable material in cases where a working-class experience was to be found. In some instances, such as Seán Mac Diarmada, there was evidence of tolerance towards Socialism—a tolerance partially induced by his own background as a migrant to Belfast, partially increased by his anxiety to place fewest ideological barriers in the way of his business of finding recruits for insurrection—but little actual understanding of it, or self-education in that respect. In other cases, the Irish Volunteers had attracted labour leaders who had fought shy of Connolly's own movement.[10]

But Connolly could hardly be absolutely sure of the I.R.B. He certainly had a very low opinion of some of its members, though not, so far as we know, of any of those in the Military Council. In his initial dealings with the I.R.B. he made his misgivings very clear to his son-in-law Archie Heron, conveying to him that

> a lot of the I.R.B. were old fogies you met in pubs and things like that, and not the kind of material that he was looking for, but when he got into closer contact he found that a new generation had come into the I.R.B. and I think that considerably changed his outlook. . . .[11]

This was a practical difficulty about his co-operation with the republican nationalists. On a theoretical level there was another barrier to be surmounted. Connolly would have had no doubt about the dedication of such veterans as Tom Clarke respecting the ideal of insurrection to bring about an Irish republic. But he knew that such men as Clarke represented that strain in republican nationalist thought which saw the nationalist objective as a political one, unconnected with social ideals. This did not prevent Clarke, like his illustrious predecessors Luby and Kickham, from being a most eloquent commentator on the social evils of his day—in particular, Clarke had written a powerful denunciation of police brutality against the workers during the great lock-out of 1913. But to Clarke, as to Luby and Kickham, devotion to national ideals had to be clear and unaffected by alien doctrines. There might be every private or public criticism to be made of the existing structure of society; but the nationalist programme must be the acquisition of a republic first, and all other questions could then be considered on their own merits. Clarke was therefore a classical example of pure revolutionary nationalism. Where he found common ground with Connolly was in his belief in the necessity for revolution, even if he saw the revolution as destined to have different consequences to those Connolly hoped for. The commitment to revolution made him a totally different proposition to such men as Arthur Griffith; but it should also be stressed that Griffith had a commitment to conservative economic thought which Clarke certainly did not.[12]

There is no more striking example of the ecumenism of the period than the readiness of Clarke and Connolly to work with one another. It was not a question of personality; no men of higher integrity existed in the Ireland of their day. But it was as hard for the straightforward political nationalist insurrectionist to throw in his lot with the revolutionary Socialist, as it was for the latter to accept alliance with the former. Both men, in their hour of crisis, showed a true greatness in their flexibility of mind on a question of co-operation which ran counter to their deepest traditions of ideology. As if that were not enough, Clarke had been as much disgusted by the sectarianism and anti-nationalist sentiment injected into Socialist ranks by Seán O'Casey as had Connolly by the sterility and imprisonment by the past which he encountered in his early dealings with the I.R.B. I have testified to Connolly's capacity for finding common ground under the most unpromising circumstances, but his normal work, in this respect, of its nature involved informing minds which were as yet not fully mature. Clarke's thought was mature, and his commitment to a purely political revolutionary nationalism was as stern and unbending as was Connolly's to the interaction of Socialism and nationalism, for Connolly, while in many respects he embodied the philosophy of the popular front, did so in a clear-cut, hard and self-conscious basis of ideology as opposed to the flabbiness which could characterise popular fronts in other times. The alliance of Clarke and Connolly, therefore, must be a testament transmitted to future generations reminding us that between the most clearly divided of doctrines there still may exist a basis for alliance. Where two such men as Clarke and Connolly could sink their great differences for a common goal, the rest of us would be well advised to think again about our points of division in which we often take so much pride.

Co-operation with Thomas MacDonagh must also have involved a similar readiness to leap barriers. In MacDonagh's case the point of division was not so much one of political *versus* social revolution, as that of a man driven at all times by awareness of social and economic necessities confronting one whose emphases were almost wholly cultural. It is clear that both cases must have involved very deliberate decisions for Connolly. For him to enter the Military Council of the I.R.B. meant coming to terms with Clarke, for Clarke was the symbol of what the Military Council meant. Clarke's 'immortal hate, and courage never to submit or yield' was an inspiration to his young colleagues as was no other human quality. A British officer was to be shot on Collins' orders during the war of 1919-21 for having insulted Clarke.[13] And the decision to draw MacDonagh into the Military Council before the Rising was one to which Connolly, now a member, was privy; and again it testifies to his ability for co-operation with men who seemed wholly different in outlook from himself. Not that the ideals in which Connolly believed were to be betrayed in the proclamation of the Irish republic which all these men signed; its text is the answer to that. But it must have seemed a long road, at times, from Connolly's first examination of his future colleagues to the issuance of that proclamation.

Connolly's resolute drive towards insurrection must not blind us to the utter hatred of war which always animated him. Physical force he had hitherto seen as only to be resorted to in circumstances of absolute extremity. In 1899 he had stated:

If the time should arrive when the party of progress finds its way to freedom barred by the stubborn greed of a possessing class entrenched behind the barriers of law and order; if the party of progress has indoctrinated the people at large with the new revolutionary conception of society and is therefore representative of the will of a majority of the nation; if it has exhausted all the peaceful means at its disposal for the purpose of demonstrating to the people and their enemies that the new revolutionary ideas do possess the suffrage of the majority; then, but not till then, the party which represents the revolutionary idea is justified in taking steps to assume the powers of government, and in using the weapons of force to dislodge the usurping class or government in possession, and treating its members and supporters as usurpers and rebels against the constituted authorities always have been treated.[14]

In passing, it may be noted how close we are here to the Catholic doctrine of 'a just war'. The extent to which Connolly rejected the physical force alternative is seldom stressed, partly because he ended his days as the leader of a violent insurrection, partly because of the militancy of his language in which his enthusiasm for economic and moral force has been misread as acceptance of physical force.

It is evident that what Connolly saw as the unprecedented character of the First World War—and its horrific character is not easy for us to realise, living as we do in an age when such horrors are commonplace—led him to alter his prerequisites for the acceptance of physical force. But before that war dawned, it may have been that Connolly's direction was even more adverse to violence than is comprehended in his statement of 1899. He was a receptive man, and numbered pacifists among his friends and associates. Certainly his initial statements on the outbreak of war make it clear that the strength of his reaction owed much to his bitter hostility to warfare of any kind. In mid-August, 1914, he said that 'this war appears to me as the most fearful crime of the centuries'.[15] In January, 1915, he reaffirmed a belief that 'war is a relic of barbarism only possible because we are governed by a ruling class with barbaric ideas'.[16] Throughout his steady movement towards insurrection he never ceased to stress that the mainspring for his new direction was the changed situation brought about by 'the carnival of murder on the continent'.[17] One regretfully parts company with Mrs Maureen Wall, author of the best essays in existence on the Easter Week Rising, when she sees Connolly as 'disillusioned by the failure of international Socialism to prevent war' and hence increasingly stressing that the cause of labour was the cause of Ireland.[18] Connolly was too old a bird to have illusions about international Socialism or Socialists, and too cosmopolitan in background to collapse into a narrow nationalism. Disgusted with the Socialists who whooped it up for war or the workers who failed to combine to end it, he certainly was, but his annoyance with them did not lead him to abandon the international factor in his Socialism. Indeed, much though Irish people tend to forget it, Connolly's decision to take up arms against the British warfare state had no mere Irish motivation. In addition to its specifically Irish goals it was also designed to furnish an example for Socialists elsewhere and to make an immediate contribution of its own to the destruction of international capitalism and of the war it had caused. The war profiteer was as much his enemy as the British overlord. Ironically, it was his very hatred of war that assisted him to accept the use of violence on his own part.

A telling but gruesome illustration of the realistic nature of his hatred for war and his awareness that his insurrection would bring its horrors in its wake is at hand. Mrs Wall has reminded us that Connolly and the other insurrection leaders 'believed that the Rising would end with close-range fighting between British and Republican forces, almost certainly with a bayonet charge', and Professor G. A. Hayes-McCoy, in an unconscious but revealing word-play, tells us that 'Connolly had a bayonet fixation'.[19] The phrase could hardly be better chosen. At the beginning of the war, Connolly, pointing to the conflict's pitting Socialist against Socialist, stated:

> When the socialist pressed into the army of the Austrian Kaiser, sticks a long, cruel bayonet-knife into the stomach of the socialist conscript in the army of the Russian Czar, and gives it a twist so that when pulled out it will pull the entrails out along with it, will the terrible act lose any of its fiendish cruelty by the fact of their common theoretical adhesion to an anti-war propaganda in times of peace?[20]

Now, the author of that sentence was no visionary. If he hated war, he did so for grimly realistic reasons. If he was prepared, at the end, to turn to violence and to lead others on a war enterprise, he was under no illusions as to what he was committing himself and his followers to. His realism dictated that he anticipate the worst; hence his stress on the ultimate horror of bayonet warfare as almost certainly in store for the insurgents. Nor would his new-found readiness to accept violence permit him to indulge in any militaristic nonsense about the sanctity of warfare. As he stated in January, 1915:

> No, there is no such thing as humane or civilised war! War may be forced upon a subject race or subject class to put an end to subjection of race, of class, or sex.

When so waged it must be waged thoroughly and relentlessly, but with no delusions as to its elevating nature, or civilising methods.[21]

Nevertheless, as Mrs Wall has so ably shown,[22] Connolly did seek to mitigate the horrors of warfare in the Rising by insisting on a defensive, and not an offensive, strategy throughout the fighting.

Mention of Mrs Wall's seminal work brings us to a final point that needs to be understood concerning Connolly and the Easter Week Rising. She has performed an invaluable service in demonstrating the limits of the importance of the I.R.B. in that event. Her essays must be read in full to grasp the strength and subtlety of her arguments, but she makes a critical synthesis in writing of Connolly and his six fellow-leaders, otherwise the Military Council of the I.R.B.:

> Although no one could possibly deny that the I.R.B. revival which had taken place in the years before 1913 had been the . . . prime factor in setting in motion the events which led up to the Rising, the fact that the seven men, who had constituted themselves a Military Council, had taken the I.R.B. oath was largely irrelevant. What was important was the fact that these men had gravitated towards each other in the years since 1913; that they shared a common ideal and a common purpose and had agreed to work together to bring about a rising. They had come to trust each other . . .[23]

It is easy, especially in an atmosphere of commemorative piety, to become excessively preoccupied by the importance of organisations. Mrs Wall's stress on the human factor takes us back to a similar stress on the part of Connolly himself. The I.R.B. was but one of many bodies and groups to which he belonged, but at no time does he seem to have allowed any organisations to obtain a place in his thought higher than its immediate utility. Political parties, and still more revolutionary groups and brotherhoods, can easily acquire a significance for their members out of all proportion to the work they perform, and thereby the factor of personal responsibility becomes eliminated. Eichmann supplies one dreadful example of such a pattern, but Irish readers will not need to look so far afield. Connolly, either in connection with the Easter Rising, or in specifically Socialist contexts, saw any organisation of which he was a member as the servant, and not the master, of his own aims and ideas. As a good ecumenist, as we have stressed, he was prepared to compromise where principle was not impaired. But he did not permit the results of such compromise to acquire an ascendancy which must either frustrate his aims or commit him to means abhorrent to his principles. Nor did he fall into the error that Seán Mac Diarmada may have failed to avoid: that of assuming that control of, or influence on, an organisation ensured complete control over its members. Connolly's evangelistic activity was always specifically among individual human beings. No organisation however impressive its cult could take the place of that.

In this connection it must also be noticed that Connolly remained impervious to the personality-cults of his day, in their nature essentially similar to the organisation-cults and equally destructive of personal intellectual and moral responsibility. Greatly though he admired the American Marxist Daniel De Leon, he had no hesitation in risking the odium of groups which had once lionised him when principle—in this case the principle of monogamy—brought him into conflict with De Leon.[24] Nor did he hesitate to criticise the charismatic James Larkin. And it is reasonable to assert that he would have had similarly little patience respecting a personality-cult for himself, requiring instead constant critical reflection on his ideas, aims and actions.

4

The Lost Heir

Not the least of the many encouraging signs given to the world during the great Dublin Labour dispute . . . was the keen and sympathetic interest shown by the 'intellectuals' in the fortunes of the workers. . . . We have no doubt that it will be found in Ireland . . . that the co-operation of the wage labourers and their intellectual comrades will create an uplifting atmosphere of social helpfulness of the greatest benefit in the work of national regeneration.[1]

Let us take one last look at Connolly and the means by which he inspired his generation before we draw a lesson from his final exercise in ideological ecumenism. Desmond Ryan's pen, as ever, captures his achievement:

> Behind the picturesque figure of Larkin rose that of James Connolly, and it was said many of the Dublin employers had come to think that in their attack upon Larkin they had called up a more deadly enemy in this quiet man with the Northern accent and the grey eyes burning with a cold, implacable light under his lofty forehead crowned with dark hair. Connolly's cold but glowing words fell on many soils: America from coast

to coast, a Glasgow street corner, an Albert Hall audience, the students of the National University, the Nationalists who still frown on Larkin, the workers of Belfast and Dublin. Even Arthur Griffith, hostile to Larkin and the Strike, admits Connolly is a man of his word, nay, the one man with a head on his shoulders amongst those Internationals, Benevolists, Foreign Emissaries and riff-raff down in Liberty Hall.[2]

His words fell on many soils. . . . And like the grain of wheat which dies, he in death can yield a far greater harvest if we will but be receptive, as he was, and not allow the thorns and bushes to destroy his message. But while we are all his legatees, we must remember that a legacy is also a very direct matter. We should consider, not merely what his legacy was, but whom he designated as the heir who would transmit it. We tend to forget that masters of thought have their executors as truly as men of more material wealth have; and the consideration of whom they appoint can tell us even more of their intentions for posterity as well as of their own priorities.

In the case of Pearse, for example, there is a very clear case of appointment of such an executor, and the significance of that appointment has not yet received the analysis it deserves. Pearse's chosen heir was of course Desmond Ryan, and much of the poverty of subsequent writing on Pearse has been occasioned by the readiness of scribes to forget this fact. Desmond Ryan in himself represented so much of what was best in Pearse, not least in the growing interest in Connolly's ideas which he was revealing by 1916. When writing on Pearse got away from Desmond Ryan, as it did in the 1930s, 1940s and 1950s, Pearse was transformed into a god. He became some remote deity, remote from investigation, remote from humanity. Yet Desmond Ryan's own brief biography of him, published within a few years of his death, refuted this nonsense in its very title—*The Man Called Pearse*. Emphasis on Pearse's humanity goes all through it, and it must remain the starting-point for any worthwhile investigation of Pearse.

Now, in the case of Connolly, can we find a similar figure? The evidence is not nearly so clear-cut. Pearse designated Desmond Ryan his literary executor in very clear terms. Connolly made no such gesture towards a fellow-soldier during the Rising. But in the last days of his life, his thoughts did turn to the future of his ideas, to the question of editing his writings, and to the propagation of his beliefs perhaps through a lecture tour in America or perhaps through organisation by his friends there. In this process, he saw one person as a critical link, a person whom he clearly felt would be his executor although he did not express the matter in the concrete terms in which Pearse designated Desmond Ryan. Yet his singling out of this man was deliberate enough. He named him—in ignorance of the fact that the man he had chosen was already dead. While Connolly's thoughts were resting on him as the future custodian of his gospel, Francis Sheehy-Skeffington lay in an unmarked grave where his murderers had thrown him after his execution in Portobello Barracks on Easter Wednesday.[3]

Nora Connolly, brave girl that she was, knew that the rules against any reference to the Rising must be broken, and precious though the few last moments with her father which officialdom granted were, she risked the loss of them to tell him the terrible truth. The shock was as unexpected as it was cruel. It must have seemed a most bitter irony that Skeffington, who had chosen peace, lay dead, while he, who had chosen war, was still surviving. It was not in Connolly's nature to despair, but the future must have seemed very bleak indeed to him as he realised what the loss of such a man would mean. With Skeffington alive, the fire of Irish Socialism would continue to burn bright; with Skeffington dead . . . Connolly does not seem to have mentioned any other name who would carry forward his message.

But his choice of Skeffington, for all that it could never be acted on, opens up a most important line of investigation to us. I have spoken of the gravity of Connolly's decisions which led to his taking part in the Rising, but we must not allow ourselves to think that these decisions dominated his attitude to the exclusion of all else. He knew that Skeffington had opposed the Rising. But Connolly was not prepared to allow his death any more than his life to come between himself and someone with whom he had a very large degree of common ground, although not necessarily complete agreement. We tend to study these men and their movements singly, we think of Skeffington in connection with women's rights and Connolly with the labour movement. We tend to forget that the men were constantly meeting, and the movements interacting. Connolly also was an advocate of women's rights; Skeffington also was a Socialist. Each man influenced the other, Connolly perhaps being the stronger force but Skeffington having a perceptible effect on Connolly too. Even at the point in their lives when their disagreement was greatest, the weeks immediately preceding the Rising, Connolly turned to Skeffington in a symbolic gesture which reveals how strongly he saw the latter as the best interpreter of his message. Connolly had written a play, and on 26 March 1916, the Workers' Dramatic Company produced and acted it in Liberty Hall. The play, *Under Which Flag?*, was primarily intended to increase the workers' solidarity with the cause of the coming Rising, and its message was therefore revolutionary nationalist. On the obvious appeal to insurrection, Francis Sheehy-Skeffington might well have been expected to turn a jaundiced eye. None the less Connolly, conscious of the need for propaganda though he was, had Skeffington review it for the playwright's own paper, *The Workers' Republic*. It was as clear an assertion as we could wish that he felt more confident of worthy judgement from Skeffington than he would from the most faithful and devoted of his personal adherents. Apart from the fact that Skeffington's accomplishments included those of dramatic criticism, and indeed of having written a play himself, Connolly knew him to be a convinced Socialist, and a determined opponent of the European war. These criteria were good enough for him—plus the fact, of course, that no more fearlessly honest a man than Skeffington lived.

The times were desperate, but they were not, I think, too desperate for Connolly to grin over the result. After some measured and well-balanced words of praise, Skeffington made an adverse criticism. Characteristically, he imported into his comment a fine piece of sardonic deflation of the hysterical anti-Germanism born of war hysteria which shrieked from every British newspaper:

The use of the soliloquy in the second act must, however, be condemned as dramatically inartistic—though Mr Connolly could plead the example of a great English dramatist who is more honoured in Germany than in his own country.[4]

It is pleasant to think of the two old friends smiling together over that little thrust. One can imagine, I think with fidelity to the realities, Skeffington taking up the point further with Connolly, and holding forth on what Ibsen would have said, and what Shaw had taught us, and how Connolly must think of this point in his next play, and Connolly listening quietly, knowing that before a month was past he would have ended forever any prospect of his writing another play, and knowing, too, that Skeffington would never agree with what he was going to do. But the Easter Rising would not divide them, any more than their views of the soliloquy did, or indeed their earlier differences had done. For their friendship, and sense of common outlook, had never weakened their capacity for criticising each other. A case in point was their disagreement on Michael Davitt.

It will be remembered that Francis Sheehy-Skeffington published in 1906 a remarkable monograph entitled *Michael Davitt: Revolutionary Agitator and Labour Leader*. It was not the young author's intention to provide anything in the nature of a biography of his subject, who had died a couple of years previously: while the narrative roughly followed the chronology of Davitt's life, this merely supplied the framework from which Skeffington was enabled to erect his real work. This was, to provide a 'primer', as he put it, of Davitt, conveying and appraising the structure of his ideas both as he enunciated them and as he sought to carry them into action. The work had a limited circulation, largely through an error in the printing arrangements, but it enjoyed an influence beyond its audience, no doubt initially because of the controversy which surrounded its inception: Skeffington was attacked by Davitt's widow, who went to great pains to make it clear that his study did not enjoy her blessing. Mrs Davitt's attitude no doubt owed something to her own somewhat rigid and unbending Catholicism of a kind whose conservatism and defensiveness contrasted with the progressivism of her husband, and Skeffington, as a Socialist, a freethinker, and an advocate of women's rights, represented forces antithetical to her views. The controversy enabled Skeffington to commence his study with a firm assertion that Davitt was not, so to speak, in private custody, but that his message existed for all who had ears to hear it, and Skeffington's own part lay in reminding his audience that Davitt's story had important lessons for the new Ireland which had survived him. Skeffington took pains to assert that he did not wish to advocate to Irish progressives that they should become intellectually imprisoned by Davitt, or that they should interpret events which would take place in the future solely by criteria formulated by Davitt in past circumstances where he was necessarily bound by environmental conditions of other days. What Skeffington wanted to do with Davitt was to use him as a means to give a sense of priorities to future Irish progressives, to demonstrate the importance of devotion to abstract ideals, to offer inspiration from his example, and to argue for the continuing significance of his social and political doctrines. Skeffington's *Davitt* remains a work of great importance today; its reissue[5] is exceptionally welcome. It may be added that Skeffington's intentions and methods in providing his Davitt primer apply with even greater force now to the maintenance of Connolly and of Skeffington himself as living forces among us.

Skeffington's service to his contemporaries and to posterity in preparing this book was at its greatest in the degree to which he thereby provided a historical background to the place of Socialism in the history of Irish ideas. Connolly immediately recognised its importance and reviewed it in detail for *The Harp*. But he saw that the enormous value of Skeffington's work could not negate certain weaknesses which arose from the writer's youthful enthusiasm. For Skeffington's *Davitt* does not represent the author at his full intellectual maturity: a close study of the work reveals to us that Skeffington's very assertiveness masks a quality of uncertainty on his own part where certain issues are concerned. It is clear, for example, that Skeffington had not yet arrived at full pacifism when he wrote that book; he would later do so.[6] Connolly did not point to the book's ambiguity on questions of recourse to arms, but his analysis did suggest a recognition that Skeffington had not arrived at a final position on certain vital questions, and that his present resting-place was not entirely a satisfactory one. Connolly saw the degree to which Skeffington's enthusiasm for Davitt could push him into the excesses of a personality cult, making him overlook too many of Davitt's blemishes. To Connolly Davitt possessed lessons not only of what to follow, but of what to avoid. On

Skeffington's own showing, Connolly pointed out, Davitt from time to time through sheer niceness of character could tend not so much to make the wrong decision as to fail to take any positive action at all. Skeffington was ready to account for Davitt's Hamlet-like behaviour as derived from a fear of weakening Irish protest through division; Connolly suggested that the problem ran deeper, and that while Davitt often saw what should be done he lacked the moral strength to do it. This comment of his tells us much of Connolly's own priorities, as well as conveying the character of his intellectual relations with Sheehy-Skeffington; he stands for us as a force of individual principle, with a great capacity for inspiring common effort and intellectual interchange. To this extent, therefore, Connolly remains a most important activist against the Irish tradition of proliferation of corrosive and destructive faction-fighting. But he also was supremely conscious of the importance of taking a stand at vital points, regardless of the possibility of alienating others. Davitt worked, as Connolly did, to create unity among different protest groups, where the initial possibility of it seemed slim; but the unity Davitt achieved was something which, in Connolly's view, he cherished to a degree where he could lose sight of essential priorities.

Oddly enough, but logically enough, Connolly had little more enthusiasm for the point in Davitt's life where he really did take a stand which played an important part in creating a split—the Parnell divorce crisis. Connolly had his own criticisms of Parnell, and plenty of them, but on this question he maintained that Skeffington was wrong to applaud Davitt for his stand. On this issue,

Connolly felt that Davitt had misread the realities of the situation; the personal factor could not be ignored in assessing what actuated Davitt, and Skeffington, in Connolly's view, should have made more of the perspective which hindsight should give him. Historically, said Connolly, it was Parnell and not Davitt who stood in favour of a truly progressive position at that moment, and who represented a realistic approach to Irish political and social questions. Davitt's standpoint was in favour of short-term political considerations; Parnell was opposing the undemocratic control of Irish protest movements by British politicians and by the Roman Catholic hierarchy. It was a position which Connolly reached by his abiding sense of historical necessities, as opposed to the more prevalent readiness to follow great men for their own sake. Of course, to support Parnell was for most men an action as deeply based on the cult of a great man as any action could be; but for the Socialist, let us remember, Davitt rather than Parnell was the great exemplar. Connolly restored a sense of history by showing that what was at stake was not whether one identified with Parnell or Davitt—who, after all, were dead; what mattered were the real issues of the past with which one was engaged—and those issues were in many ways still very much alive. Davitt, from the Socialist standpoint, might have been a very nice chap on any estimation; Parnell, again from that standpoint, was in many respects not a nice chap at all. But what was involved was not whether chaps were nice chaps, but how the issue read when placed in its historical context, and on this showing, the split made for a situation where Parnell was right and Davitt was wrong. One may remark that it was this attitude on Connolly's part to history which did so much to emancipate both Irish historical writing in general, and the deployment of history in the Irish progressive cause in particular, from the personality cult, and to give them a far more valid meaning where the emphasis was on how the economic and social destinies of the people at large were affected by events. It has been argued that Connolly, and Marxist historians in general, focused attention on economic forces, at the expense of understanding the human spirit; the truth is in fact that Connolly—and other Marxist historians, when they are intelligent Marxists and good historians—took attention away from one or two persons and restored an emphasis on all persons. It is childish to argue that we are coming to terms with the human spirit when our focus is on one or two human spirits to the exclusion of all the rest. Connolly, most notably in his *Labour in Irish History*, brought the people back into Irish history. It may be added that he did so seeking to inspire further work, not to lay down a dogma to bind posterity. For Connolly's thought was, as he saw it, to be a beginning of further reflection and action, not an end to it. And it was in this spirit that he criticised Skeffington, with a view to influencing his future work and to prompting further intellectual exchanges.

I have concentrated on Connolly's criticisms of Skeffington's work in order to show the confrontation of their minds; but I must stress above all that the overriding spirit of Connolly's review, a spirit which transcended his article at every point, was one of the greatest applause for Skeffington's achievement. The differences between these men were differences based on immense intellectual respect for one another; and the points of agreement were so many that Connolly had little need to stress them, as he would have stressed them had there been fewer of them. Skeffington saw their relationship in similar terms. A most interesting letter from him survives from 1911, in which he conveys what Connolly meant to him. It is with much amusement that I record the name of the letter's recipient: Bourgeois.[7]

1911 is in many ways far from us, but in some respects it presents situations very familiar indeed. The Skeffington-Bourgeois correspondence is a case in point. Bourgeois, it appears, was writing a thesis, and was enthusiastically seeking new leads on his material. The thesis, as it happened, was not a bad one for the day, and was published by Constable in 1913 under the title *John Millington Synge and the Irish National Theatre*. As far as his method of research was concerned, Bourgeois seems quickly to have grasped the point which many commentators have missed—that the Dublin cultural community perpetually involved wholly unexpected points of contact between persons of apparently very different outlook and interest. He perceived that there were associations between the Abbey Theatre and Socialists, and the next stage was for him to investigate Irish Socialism, with the assistance of his correspondent Skeffington. Skeffington suggested that Fred Ryan would be of use and . . .

> Practically all Irish Socialists, however, are organised in the Socialist Party of Ireland. This Party meets in the Antient Concert Buildings, 42 E. Great Brunswick Street, Dublin; it also has branches in Belfast and Cork.

The Dublin body holds public meetings, at the address named every Sunday at eight p.m.; also out of door meetings, in Foster Place, the Phoenix Park, etc.; also economic classes every Wednesday at eight. I should recommend you to go to some of these meetings, and ask for Mr James Connolly, the Organizer. He knows more about Irish Socialism than anyone else, having founded the first Socialist Party in Dublin nearly twenty years ago. Originally it was called the Socialist Republican Party, and was very extreme. It had many vicissitudes and the usual quantity of splits. Two years ago it was reorganised on a new and broader basis, and is making considerable progress.

At the Antient Concert Buildings you can also get the pamphlets published by this Party in its various phases.

Irish Socialism is not at all agrarian—mainly industrial, with a considerable intellectual wing, which, however, is not active in the propaganda.

I hope these few hints will put you on the right track. I shall be glad to supplement them, so far as I am able, on any other points you wish to ask about. But if you go down to the Antient Concert Buildings to-night and see Connolly, and if you afterwards communicate with Ryan, I think you will be able to get the fullest particulars from them as to Irish Socialism, past, present, and future.

We perceive at once from this document that Skeffington had diagnosed a growth in receptivity on the part of Connolly's movement, and that he himself had been very conscious of the efforts Connolly had made to combat sectarianism and increase his area of influence and potential recruitment. It is also clear that Skeffington responded to these efforts very warmly. His own work to win votes for women and accomplish various social reforms brought him increasingly to the side of Connolly, and while neither man lost sight of the ultimate Socialist goal, both were prepared to struggle for short-term achievements which would improve the lot of those whose cause they had taken up. The one point at which real difference existed in the end was on the question of insurrection by violence.[8]

I have selected what seem to me some of the most symbolic moments of the interaction of these two remarkable men—Skeffington's review of Connolly's play in 1916, Connolly's critique of Skeffington's book in 1908, Skeffington's letter to Bourgeois in 1911—but I would be doing a disservice were my stress on these to distract attention from the day-to-day pattern of their association. It was clearly a deepening friendship and a progressive mutual stimulation. But even in the earliest stage it is evident that Connolly had some notion of Skeffington in a role which anticipated that of literary executor. In 1909 Connolly knew Skeffington much less well than he was afterwards to do, and felt less justification for assuming that Skeffington would undertake the apostleship of his message than he was to feel in 1916. Nevertheless in that year we find him writing from the U.S.A. to William O'Brien concerning the book publication of the articles he had written on *Labour in Irish History*:

... you mentioned Sheehy-Skeffington .... It occurred

to me that you might ask him would he be willing, if I sent him the manuscript of the book, to introduce it to some London publisher for me . . . If he did, his introduction would go a long way to secure a reading and perhaps acceptance. . . . tell our comrade that I do not ask him to endorse the book, but only to recommend it as a contribution to an unexploited side of Irish history and literature.[9]

O'Brien had mentioned Skeffington's having joined the Socialist Party of Ireland, as a result of which, states O'Brien in his memoirs, 'the membership was very different to what we had been in the habit of getting in the socialist movement prior to that'.[10] Skeffington was, in fact, to prove the advance guard of intellectuals' involvement in the Dublin working-class movement, an involvement which swelled dramatically in the crisis of the 1913 lock-out. In view of the inflated rhetoric which can emanate from Popular Front groups on the interaction of intellectuals and workers, it is instructive to examine a very genuine interaction.

Francis Sheehy-Skeffington, as a vigorous and active Socialist, supplied a critical link between British and Irish Socialist journalism through his paper the *Irish Citizen*, and through his Dublin representation of the *Daily Herald*; his role in this respect was the more important after W. P. Ryan, editor of the *Irish Peasant* and father of Desmond Ryan, had returned to Britain. Ryan supplied the main thrust of left-wing journalism in Ireland in the first decade of the twentieth century: Skeffington and Connolly divide the honours between them for the period 1910–1916. Necessarily, the relations between

Skeffington and Connolly could be inhibited by this: Connolly, as a labour organiser, sometimes needed to be highly diplomatic in his dealings with British comrades—although he seems to have enjoyed publicly relieving his feelings when diplomacy had ended—and Skeffington, rightly, saw his special position on the *Daily Herald* as a means of telling home-truths about British comrades in their own back-yard. Later, for even more obvious reasons, Connolly had to exclude Skeffington from his confidence respecting his plans for insurrection. But the co-operation between both men on the essential critical questions of Socialism continued unabated.

Francis Sheehy-Skeffington's outstanding contribution to Irish Socialism was of course his stress on the rights of women. We cannot now assess—and we may never know—the degree to which he influenced Connolly in this respect. The most probable answer is that Skeffington sharpened and strengthened, by his constant stress on the matter, a hitherto existing commitment in this respect in Connolly's mind. What is certain is that Connolly seems to have made himself much more conscious of the rights of women than were most Socialist writers of his day. To them, it was a creed to which most of them gave lip-service. Connolly explored the matter in great depth, and returned to it again and again. The notable case is Chapter VI of *The Re-Conquest of Ireland,* entitled 'Woman':

> Upon woman, as the weaker physical vessel, and as the most untrained recruit, the struggle was inevitably the most cruel ... Rebellion, even in thought, produces a mental atmosphere of its own; the mental atmosphere

the women's rebellion produced, opened their eyes and trained their minds to an understanding of the effects upon their sex of a social system in which the weakest must inevitably go to the wall, and when a further study of the capitalist system taught them that the term 'the weakest' means in practice the most scrupulous, the gentlest, the most humane, the most loving and compassionate, the most honourable, and the most sympathetic, then the militant women could not fail to see, that capitalism penalised in human beings . . . those characteristics of which women supposed themselves to be the most complete embodiment. . . . The worker is the slave of capitalist society, the female worker is the slave of that slave. In Ireland that female worker has hitherto exhibited, in her martyrdom, an almost damnable patience. . . . Of what use to such sufferers can be the re-establishment of any form of Irish State if it does not embody the emancipation of womanhood.[11]

But he was to return to the point again and again. We saw above how in 1915 he spoke of the subjection of race, or class, or sex,[12] clearly equating all three as crimes calling for redress, and also holding all three to be interconnected. It did not, of course, rest purely with Skeffington to keep Connolly afire on the question. Apart from his own instincts Connolly's observation of the increasing participation of women in Irish life underlined the significance of what was involved. Skeffington would not have approved of one result of the fact: that, as Mrs Maureen Wall has noted, the fight for women's rights was not without its importance indirectly in influencing the attitude of wives, mothers and sisters, who encouraged their men-folk to answer the call when the time for action came, and more directly in placing women in prominent roles in nursing, catering, secretarial and communication services, and even in the fighting line itself, while the Rising was in progress.[13]

Connolly, as I say, needed little reminder of the importance of women's militancy when one considers that his earliest days in Dublin involved working alongside Maud Gonne, afterwards MacBride, and his later years brought him Constance Markiewicz as a colleague. But he parallels Skeffington's urgency on the matter, and, given that it was impossible to be in Skeffington's company without finding oneself discussing the question, given that Connolly regularly read Skeffington's incessant writing on the issue, given that Connolly's sense of the matter's priority seems similar to Skeffington's, there seems a clear case of the fruit of their co-operation.

It is important to note that Skeffington's pacifism did not divide him from Connolly until very late in their association. Skeffington thoroughly supported Connolly on the hatefulness of the First World War, and while he would reject the assumption that its holocaust could only be answered by violence, the initial stage of their opposition to the war brought them closer together. Both men found themselves in increasing conflict with the authorities, particularly in their struggles against recruiting. Admittedly, Connolly had been a marked man since the 1913 lock-out and Skeffington at the same time was fast coming to be regarded as a comparably reprehensible enemy of Law and Order. When William O'Brien was arrested in the months before the outbreak of war, the warder remarked pleasantly: 'We had Connolly and Larkin up here before; we're expecting Skeffington any day.'[14] In 1915 they realised their expectations, Skeffington being arrested for anti-recruiting speeches a short time after Seán Mac Diarmada had been jailed for the same offence (albeit with different motivation). It will be recalled that Skeffington embarked on a hunger-and-thirst strike, and was released after a week of torture. However differently Connolly and Skeffington might ultimately choose to react to the war, Connolly was under no illusions as to the integrity of Skeffington's opposition to that war.

Skeffington's awareness of the increasing depth of the workers' struggle against capitalism and warfare led him to become a member of the committee of the Irish Citizen Army, although he must certainly have done so in a spirit of hoping for the workers' involvement together as a force for moral resistance to police brutality. In 1914 the Irish Neutrality League was formed with Connolly as President and Skeffington as a member of that committee also; it was a body whose programme outlined non-violent means of opposing the war, although behind the scenes it seems—unknown to Skeffington—to have been influenced by I.R.B. men with very different ultimate aims.[15] One plan, which has been seen as a forerunner to the Easter Week Rising, took the form of seizing and holding the Mansion House in Dublin to prevent a recruiting meeting there which Asquith was to have addressed. The plan fell through when it was discovered that governmental authorities already were in position there, but Skeffington volunteered for the engagement. What is perplexing is the suggestion those who took the Mansion House were to 'hold it and fight, if necessary, to the last man', which hardly seems a Skeffingtonian course of action. Indeed, it makes no sense. The truth would seem to be either that the entire exercise was intended to be a demonstration of moral force which, in the aftermath of the Rising, has been misread as one of physical force—misread, and, it is possible, deliberately misremembered by activists seeking to give the Rising additional credentials by pointing to earlier efforts along the same lines—or else that the non-violent element in the Irish Neutrality League were being deceived by some of their colleagues and by I.R.B. men in the background who intended to turn a moral force exercise into an armed clash.[16] The latter is possible from what we know of the infiltration, open-front-and-secret-conspiracy, and takeover tactics brought to a fine art by Seán Mac Diarmada, but as against this it is important to note that in his early writings after the outbreak of war, Connolly spoke far more in terms of economic and social resistance to the warfare state rather than of a physical force response. One cannot be too explicit about it, since at this point he is clearly giving notice that physical force is no longer only the remotest of options, but it is still not in the forefront of his argument. At all events, in Citizen Army and in Mansion House Committee, Connolly had seen Skeffington oppose the world war to the fullest degree compatible with his pacifism. In the latter part of 1915 and early 1916, both men acknowledged that their ways had divided.

Skeffington publicly and privately deplored the growing move towards militarism in Irish nationalist and Socialist circles and communicated his anxiety to Larkin in the U.S.A. and to William O'Brien in Dublin.[17] Skeffington must have caught something of what was in the wind when on Easter Sunday, 1916, he visited Liberty Hall as he so frequently did. In its way that visit also was symbolic. Skeffington could not support Connolly's decision to take up arms, but he did not see that as any reason to cut himself off from Liberty Hall.[18]

So the appointment of his executor does everything to confirm the picture we have been forming of Connolly. The Rising was of course the greatest thing in his last years, yet he was prepared to set it aside as a criterion in the appointment of a critical person to further his doctrines. It was in his nature to accept a common ground, and if the ground in common was greater in extent than the ground in dispute, he was not prepared to lose good allies on major questions because of rigid dogmatism on lesser ones. And again, the choice of Skeffington reminds us that we, who have perhaps treated the Rising as the high point in all Irish history past, present and future, are here reminded by Connolly that it was but one means to an end, and that the end was of far greater importance. From this standpoint the choice of Skeffington may well have been an action of Connolly's of greater ultimate significance than his death, since it testified to the way in which he hoped to shape the future communication of his doctrines. His choice tells us once more how in social thought as well as in Catholicism, he was an ecumenist. But even more does it tell us of the great significance he placed in integrity, in moral and physical courage, in endless zeal for the improvement of mankind, in gentleness and receptivity and readiness to learn—and in a capacity to laugh[19]—all of them qualities so much to the fore in the character of Francis Sheehy-Skeffington.

I may observe in conclusion that the decision—the natural impulse—to make Skeffington his future evangelist also suggests that Connolly was by no means so committed to the use of force as has been suggested. I do not mean that he repudiated his decision to lead an insurrection; he never did that. But it suggests he was rather more open-minded on the merits of appeal to violence than he is generally assumed to have been.

5

Connolly and Ourselves

I will say a prayer for all brave men who do their duty according to their lights.[1]

In sum, then, Connolly's life must be an inspiration to us, in what he thought, in his triumph over economic hardship and its normal product—despair—and in the way he studied, worked and lived among his fellows. In particular, his style in propaganda and in action offers us an example. His final sacrifice cannot be fully understood unless it is seen not only as testimony to the dedication which his ideals demanded, but also of readiness to co-operate and ignore significant—but not overwhelming—points of doctrinal difference with votaries of other causes. His capacity for exploiting common ground and his hatred of hair-splitting have lessons for those who believe in ideals but who succumb to the dangers he learned to avoid through experience, such as becoming absorbed in splits or in excessive devotion or opposition to single personalities. And however zealous a Socialist and a nationalist Connolly may have been, he also reminds us that absolute rigidity of doctrine becomes intellectually self-destructive when it leads to social exclusiveness or weakens absolute freedom of association. His great work in finding and exploiting common ground in favour of the quest for social justice must also be seen as a peculiarly remarkable achievement when one considers the brilliance and individuality of the men and women to whom he appealed in that incredibly exciting generation.

We will indeed be a remarkable people if we can produce anything to equal Connolly's generation. We will be even more remarkable if we can produce anything to equal Connolly himself. But, however much we may honestly admit ourselves to fall short of these goals, we will still have done well if we try to follow the morals to be drawn from his life, work and thought. We will begin to apply these morals when we first succeed in being less conceited about how far we have come today. We can learn from Connolly's awareness of the significance of economic forces in history, and realise that such petty progress as we have in fact made has been substantially the product of outside events and one owing very little to ourselves. To be sure, we have come some distance from the material conditions of Connolly's day, and from the horror that was industrial society as he knew it. We can see improvement in the ghastly environment of the Belfast and Dublin workers whom Connolly represented, and whose experience made his aims in the 1916 insurrection far more of a reality than the theories and near-dreams that animated his fellow-leaders. The condition of the working class was one Irish question which the British had not even begun to answer, and Home Rule would not have solved it. But how well have we—as opposed to our environmental conditions—

succeeded in solving it? The point for us to bear in mind, in all humility, is not how far we have come from Connolly's day, but how very small a distance it really has been when set alongside what could have been done and what Connolly asked that we should do.[2]

Let us never forget that Connolly sought to found a Socialist Ireland, a workers' republic. That ideal still lies before us, unrealised and widely unacknowledged. He hoped to eliminate the ideal of competition and to instil instead a sense of co-operation, a true fellowship, a true brotherhood, a true intellectual climate of free and incessant exchange of debate and idea, such as he himself created among his associates and sought to increase elsewhere. He sought to destroy the gospel of greed and the ideal of acquisitiveness and substitute instead a general belief in man's partnership with his fellow-man. And since, in our brave new world of today, many who lack the optimism that was his tell us that human nature makes such an ideal impossible, let us turn to him for the last word on that point. The student of political theory will see the obligations to Marx in the passage I am about to quote, and he should also see the influence of St Thomas More's *Utopia*:

> Men and women are at all times zealous for honour, for the esteem of their fellows, and when the hope of plunder is removed out of the field of human possibility those specially gifted ones who now exhaust their genius in an effort to rule, will as vehemently exert themselves to win the honour accorded to those who serve.

Epilogue: Connolly 1968 and 1971

> ... if I were asked what statement of Irish policy was most in accord with my view as to what human beings should struggle for, I would stand side by side with James Connolly.
>
> Eamon de Valera, 29 April 1932

In the opening words of the preceding lecture, delivered nearly three years ago, I cited the work of the Americans in preparing authoritative texts of the writings of their honoured dead, and suggested Connolly was a natural subject for similar treatment from us. Now, I wonder whether another enterprise is not even more necessary Some years ago Professor Merrill Peterson produced a remarkable work entitled *The Jefferson Image in the American Mind* which told of the uses to which Americans of widely differing views and creeds had put their dead Jefferson. A study of Connolly's reputation might also reveal very startling uses to which Irishmen and others have put Connolly. It would in many ways make sad reading, at points reminiscent of Brecht's play 'St Joan of the Stockyards' where the heroine is canonised against her will by those who intend to destroy her real legacy.

But such a work would also be the record of persons who sought to perpetuate that legacy. At many points their use of Connolly would reveal a different kind of irony, one whereby, in some cases, Connolly's inspirational words became a prelude to the ossification of thought and action rather than the further stimulus he intended. And there would also be those who learned to cite Connolly with a view to furthering aims of a variety and an irrelevance in the pursuit of which all texts, from the Bible onward, have been cited. Another form of irony would emerge in the assessment of commemorative celebrations which had the unexpected effect of reactivating the memory of Connolly in new ways. I myself was the victim of one such irony. Thinking about Connolly in 1968 I saw aspects of his legacy which might rekindle old sentiments in the framework of Irish politics which I still saw in a traditional way. What I did not anticipate was the rebirth of Connolly in a global outburst of participation politics, whose advocates in Ireland, especially in Northern Ireland, proclaimed it with stress on Connolly's teachings and reaffirmed his powerful relevance to the establishment against which they struggled. Connolly between 1968 and 1971 moved from the lecture-room to the streets, and the insights his writings exhibited in the analysis of industrial Ulster proved all too relevant in the work commenced by courageous young people no longer content to leave Connolly in the shrine of inactive piety to which he had been consigned by their cautious seniors.

It was curious, too, that the new place of Connolly as inspiration for this very different younger generation should have coincided with his final abandonment by the Fianna Fáil government. In my lecture I sought to give credit for sincerity to a ruling group whose interpretation had, in my view, parted company from reality: but the more recent attitude, insincere though it is in many respects, has certainly been honest in its utter break with a past commitment to social revolution, violent or non-violent as it might be. It was curious that the apotheosis, intended to have been set on foot in 1966 which would have left the leaders of 1916 as venerable and as harmless as mummies outside of a horror film, resulted instead in a dramatically increased interest in the living Connolly. By the time I delivered my lecture, this process was well under way, and it was clear to me that the commemoration of which I was asked to form a part, was solidly on the side of a living Connolly. If the government by 1971 had clearly decided that Connolly and others like him were too combustible for further safe use, the Labour party in the same period was being stimulated to revitalise Connolly's legacy. It may be argued that in doing so it showed weaknesses; Connolly's most genuine heirs within its ranks had yet to ponder the lessons of his anti-sectarianism in the political context, while others had much to learn concerning the importance of anti-sectarianism in racial and religious matters. Connolly's pattern of principle combined with receptive evangelisation was not an easy one to follow. But at least the Labour party was now confronting real dilemmas, instead of sweeping them aside by means of honorific platitudes.

If the years between 1968 and 1971 confirmed that Ireland was to reckon in the foreseeable future with cults of a living as opposed to a dead Connolly, it would be a foolish man who assumed a blessing from Connolly for all forms of new vitality. There was nothing in his career which could be cited in favour of political adventurism. That he finally took to the gun is undeniable; but he did so as an absolute and final act, and did so himself, not by means of pawns destined for cannon-fodder. He had scant use for politicians seeking to exploit gun-toting in his own day, and he confronted them in the shape of the Tories and Unionists who sponsored the Ulster Volunteers. But the political adventurers of modern Ireland, like their belated governmental critics, acknowledged that Connolly's agitation of social questions was of little service to them. The intensity of the effort made in Dublin governmental and ex-governmental circles to preach a nationalism untainted by any suggestion that Northern Ireland's woes were social, was in itself testimoney to the fear in which Connolly's legacy was coming to be held.

It was essential that the cult of a living Connolly would also demand an increasingly critical view of him. He himself would be the last writer to seek endorsement of his every word and action, particularly in that his life was one long essay in self-education. His message does not depend on closing eyes to subsequent advances in knowledge. We may wish, and we should wish, to reaffirm our faith in his anti-imperialist principles, but in the light of later wisdom, we should do so with a clearer eye to those for whom we testify. The Boers look different in our day from what they appeared to him; and there are modern Boers, in other latitudes, whom we should view with similar caution, however repulsive we find their oppressors. We owe unbending allegiance to his conviction that the nation must be imbued with social justice; but this does not mean that we should create, as Connolly tended to create, a Paradise under the name of pre-Norman Ireland. He would like us better if we tried to implement, and thus to improve on, his own realistic standards, and hence to say that the Ireland of the first millennium A.D. with its vast numbers of slaves must take a different shape in the minds of future historians of labour in Irish history. We should admire the courage that led him into the Easter Rising; we may wish to applaud its ideals; that does not involve our offering it an otiose and possibly ill-advised posthumous endorsement. He did what he thought right; that is no reason why we should abandon the faculty of human intellect in the conviction that he has done enough thinking for all of us.

If they are wise, this and later generations will return to Connolly. And, if their wisdom can transcend the petty wisdom of self-interest, they will go forth from his works with a new clarity of thought and a new radicalism of action. But only by its being theirs, taken in the context of their times and applied with their advantages, can it also be his and thus come closer to realising his aims. Finally, it must be undertaken with laughter and constant self-mockery. If in a sense of righteousness we give ourselves airs, let us remember that in this we are departing hopelessly from the precept and practice of James Connolly.

Notes

CHAPTER 1

[1] Connolly, 'Changes', 9 May 1914, in Desmond Ryan, ed., *The Workers' Republic*, Dublin 1951, 161–2.

[2] C. Desmond Greaves, *The Life and Times of James Connolly*, London 1961. I have drawn much more heavily on this book than these notes indicate. See also the files of the *Irish Democrat* (London), especially since the publication of Mr Greaves' book; he has from time to time made additional contributions to the subject in articles for that journal.

[3] Desmond Ryan, *James Connolly—His Life Work and Writings* with a preface by H. W. Nevinson, Dublin 1924. See also the same writer's final estimate of Connolly, corrected by him for the printers but published after his death: Desmond Ryan, 'James Connolly' in J. W. Boyle, ed., *Leaders and Workers*, Cork n.d.

[4] Desmond Greaves has suggested to me that W. P. Ryan, who also wrote under the Irish form of his name (Liam P. Ó Riain), was initially asked to write the book, and that his son then agreed to take over the task together with his father's research notes. W. P. Ryan, *The Irish Labour Movement*, Dublin n.d., is of course an invaluable pioneer work by a journalist of major significance in Connolly's generation, for a sketch of whom see Brian Inglis, 'Moran of the *Leader* and Ryan of the *Irish Peasant*' in Conor Cruise O'Brien, ed., *The Shaping of Modern Ireland*, London 1960.

[5] Nora Connolly O'Brien, *Portrait of a Rebel Father*, Dublin 1935; see also *The Unbroken Tradition*, New York 1918, by the same author.

[6] London 1934. Desmond Ryan enjoys the distinction of not only being the author of the most valuable and most remarkable memoir of the period, but of also being the writer of the best historical monograph on the Rising itself—*The Rising*, Dublin 1949.

[7] *The Social Teachings of James Connolly*, Dublin 1920, a work of remarkable insight, with some points of interpretation requiring modification following the passage of time. It is hoped that a critical edition will shortly be published.

[8] *Labour in Ireland*, Dublin n.d., consists of *Labour in Irish History* (Dublin 1910) and *The Re-Conquest of Ireland* (Dublin 1915), together with an introduction by Cathal O'Shannon. The other volumes required a major task in selection, compilation and cross-reference, the last being of particular value. They are: *Socialism and Nationalism*, Dublin 1948, introduction by Desmond Ryan; *Labour and Easter Week 1916*, Dublin 1949, introduction by William O'Brien; *The Workers' Republic*, Dublin 1951, introduction by William McMullen. A recent popular anthology, of useful character though unsightly production, is *The Best of Connolly*, ed. Proinsias Mac Aonghusa and Liam Ó Réagáin, Cork 1967; its title is of course pejorative nonsense.

[9] 'The Irish Socialist Library', in particular, has done good service in making Connolly's writings available in pamphlet form and at very modest prices. See particularly *Erin's Hope* and *The New Evangel*, with introductions by J. Deasy, Dublin 1968, and the recent excellent collection of Connolly's articles on insurrectionary warfare issued by New Books Publications (with introduction by Michael O'Riordan) as *Revolutionary Warfare*, Dublin 1968.

[10] The inevitable answer to any proposal such as this is that the Russians and Americans have the money to do it, and we have not. We have the money, in fact, but official deployment of it for commemorative purposes has hitherto been directed to symbolise the deaths of the nation's founders rather than to

perpetuate their teachings. Private persons, or, as in the case of the Ryan selections from Connolly, specific bodies such as—in that instance—the Irish Transport and General Workers' Union, have met the cost involved. It is time that a national effort should be made. It is also clear from the example of the volumes edited by Desmond Ryan, so magnificently produced at the Sign of the Three Candles, that we have traditions of book preparation which can stand comparison with those of any country.

[11] See *Trade Union Information,* issued by Irish Congress of Trade Unions, April 1968, 6–7. Mr Nevin's services to Connolly scholarship have been of great benefit to me in the preparation of this lecture. I would wish particularly to stress his essay 'The Irish Citizen Army' in O. Dudley Edwards and Fergus Pyle, ed., *1916: The Easter Rising,* London 1968, and his recent broadcast talk on Connolly which will, no doubt, be published shortly as is customary for these Thomas Davis lectures of which it is one. Mr Nevin's broadcast was delivered on 27 October 1968, and I was unable to hear it; but for the revisal of this lecture for publication I have been enabled to draw on the very full report of it given in the *Irish Times* of the following day.

[12] Quoted in Ryan, *Remembering Sion,* 171.

[13] The speech in question was delivered on 18 February 1966. I take my text from the *Irish Times* report of the next day.

[14] *Social Teachings of Connolly,* 10–12.

[15] One problem about getting to terms with Connolly's generation has arisen from the fact that most of the leading historical treatments of it are in fact publications of these Thomas Davis Lectures. These are splendid so far as they go; but we must not assume that they take the place of the ultimate syntheses. It is also true that the broadcast talk imposes a rigidity on the lecturer which may liberate him from the discursiveness of which ordinary lectures, like this one, are rather too full, but which at the same time requires a focus that may prove somewhat distorting. The leading volumes which cover the principal figures of the period are Cruise O'Brien ed. *Shaping of Modern Ireland;* Desmond

Williams, ed., *The Irish Struggle 1916–1926*, London 1966; and F. X. Martin, O.S.A., ed., *Leaders and Men of the Easter Rising*, London 1967. Of these the first and the last give impressive treatments of one or two notable figures in each lecture, but the interaction of all of these remarkable participants necessarily becomes obscured, especially where it exists as a simple fact of life rather than as the immediate origin of great events. All the editors make some efforts to draw the threads of their story together, Conor Cruise O'Brien's pioneer essay 'Ireland 1891–1916' in the volume edited by him being still of vital importance: but the signposts he set up in that essay have not been followed to the necessary extent. Professor Williams' collection lies largely outside the Connolly era in time, but in its first essay, by Professor Martin, it also seeks to produce a synthesis: the result is most helpful, but is still more the individual parts than the sum of these parts, and the author's very relevant stress on the ultimate recourse to violence—relevant in view of the theme and focus of the Williams book—tends to weaken the significance of pre-insurrection Irish cultural society as something to be considered for its own sake. It must also be added that while these books are impressive, the essays are far from uniform in quality, nor is the extent of the enquiry comprehensive. Seán O'Casey forms a very odd omission from these lectures; and it still remains the case that nothing of real value has been written about Joseph Plunkett: to take only two examples.

[16]This point was made more clumsily in the original lecture, and Mr Ailfrid Mac Lochlainn pointed out to me afterwards that I erred in suggesting Connolly was a product of his generation instead of being primarily an influence on it. 'Dublin was a seedbed of conflicting ideologies as you say', he said, 'but Connolly, as you yourself indicate, was out of it for most of the time.' I have revised this passage accordingly; at the same time, while Connolly's influence on his Dublin contemporaries clearly far outweighed their ideological effect on him, we must not assume the situation to have been a one-way traffic purely.

[17] The italics are mine, inserted to show where the emphasis must be placed in reading the poem. It is clear from the poem as a whole that whatever AE's reservations about the insurrection and its leaders may have been, he indicates very strongly that Connolly was the only insurgent leader he commemorates whom he had accepted before the Rising, as possessing a viable philosophy. It is interesting to note that the poem as originally constructed was purely a memorial to the insurgent dead, and that before 1918 was out, AE revised it to include notable Irishmen who had died in British service in the world war—a change of emphasis wrought by what seemed to him a repudiation of the latter's sacrifice by the Ireland of his day. At the same time he deleted a verse on the imprisoned Constance Markiewicz. The original version was privately published by Clement Shorter, who went in a lot for private printing and was son-in-law to Dr George Sigerson of the I.R.B. The final text is frequently reprinted without the material on the men who died in the British trenches—surely a contradiction of AE's ultimate purpose of demonstrating the varieties of nationalist response to the war. The correct final version is less frequently quoted; its most recent appearance is in Edwards and Pyle, ed., *1916*.

[18] Geraldine Plunkett Dillon, in 'Joseph Plunkett', no. 7 of the Telefís Éireann series on the signatories of the Proclamation of the Easter Rising shown throughout Easter Week, 1966, produced by Aindreas Ó Gallchoir under the general title *On Behalf of the Provisional Government*. I have found this series a most valuable compilation of significant evidence on the insurgent leaders and their contemporaries; it consisted entirely of the evidence of surviving witnesses. I am also much obliged to the producer for his inspiration during the period when I had the privilege of giving him some small assistance in the preparation of the films.

[19] Interview of the present writer with James Doherty, January 1966. Mr Doherty was a Belfast docker and organiser who worked closely with both men during their Belfast days.

[20] *Social Teachings of Connolly*, 8.

[21] The best memoir of Connolly's American experience is

that which appears in the autobiography of the great American labour leader Elizabeth Gurley Flynn, *I Speak My Own Piece*, New York 1955. For a scientific modern analysis of the labour crises and movements there in which he played a part, see Patrick Renshaw, *The Wobblies—The Industrial Workers of the World*, London 1967, especially pp. 166–7, on Connolly's attitude in the controversies and questions of policy; pp. 276–9, making a general point on the international character of Connolly's work in Ireland; and p. 284, throwing an interesting light on Connolly's posthumous influence in Australia. Mr Greaves has much of value to say on Connolly's American years. My data on Belfast are drawn from a multitude of sources, but some excellent background is provided by the writings of Dr J. W. Boyle, and the appendix to Emmet Larkin, *James Larkin*, Cambridge, Mass. 1964.

[22] Ryan, *Remembering Sion*, 57–8.

[23] *The Harp* (Jan. 1908). Few of the articles in this publication were actually signed by Connolly, but it has become possible to assert which of the unsigned pieces were definitely his as a result of the identification made by the late William O'Brien.

[24] *The Harp* (March 1908).
[25] *The Harp* (April 1908).
[26] *Ibid*.
[27] *The Harp* (Nov. 1909).

CHAPTER 2

[1] Connolly, 'Labour, Nationality and Religion', 1910, in Ryan, ed., *The Workers' Republic*, 193–4.

[2] *Social Teachings of Connolly*, 12.

[3] Leading article in *The Workers' Republic*, 29 Jan. 1916, quoted in full in the appendix to McKenna, *Social Teachings of Connolly*, 47–9, and reprinted in Desmond Ryan, ed., *The Workers' Republic*, 188–90, under the title 'The Programme of Labour'. By a printer's error the date of the article is given as '19 Jan.' in the latter; Father McKenna has the correct date,

but his printer has made the republic of the newspaper title that of 'the worker' and not of 'the workers'.

[4] *The Harp* (Jan. 1909). Those interested in checking this extract against its scriptural antecedent may care to examine Matthew 21:12–13; Mark 11:15–18; Luke 19:45–46; John 2:13–17. Mark 11:18 is of particular interest in this connection, forging as it does, a direct link between Christ's action on this occasion and the conspiracy to have him crucified. The efforts of William Martin Murphy's subordinates to ensure that James Connolly would be shot has a strange echo of this also: see Edwards and Pyle, ed., *1916*, appendix II. Jeremiah 7:11 is of course an important anticipation of the denunciation of the money-changers and can readily be applied to the corruption of religion by capitalism.

[5] Thomas Bell, *Pioneering Days*, pp. 51 ff., quoted in Ryan, ed., *Workers' Republic*, 61, note 2.

[6] Connolly, Roman Catholicism and Socialism' in Ryan, ed., *The Workers' Republic*, 56. See also pp. 57–60.

[7] Connolly, 'Labour, Nationality and Religion', in Ryan, ed., *The Workers' Republic*, 263–4. This is from the concluding paragraphs of the famous reply to the Lenten sermons of the Rev. Robert Kane, S.J., in 1910.

[8] John Higham, *Strangers in the Land—Patterns of American Nativism*, New Brunswick, N.J., 1955. See also my own article 'Nativism (American)' in *New Catholic Encyclopedia*. A distinguished economist of British domicile but Hungarian origin noted the same point about the British which Higham and I have made in the American context, and was quoted to this effect in the *Observer* 'Sayings of the Year' for 1968: 'It is only since the British lost their self-confidence that they have become xenophobic.' Lord Balogh (formerly Professor Thomas Balogh) was very rightly drawing a distinction between the previously existing general concepts of British ethnic superiority which did not carry with them the present day features of fear and hatred, and those prevailing today. His remarks would of course have to be qualified, in that in former years certain sectors of British society were lacking in confidence and their attitudes may be seen as precursors of

the more widely-held sentiment of today, e.g. the exploited British working class of the last century naturally included many pockets of utter lack of self-confidence and hence xenophobia, as expressed, for example, against Catholics in general and Irish immigrants in particular, in ways similar to what is found today against non-white Commonwealth immigrants.

[9]The reader who wishes to examine such literature might turn to the files of the Irish *Catholic Bulletin*. It must be realised that this diseased mentality co-existed with the great intellectual excitement of Connolly's outstanding intellectual contemporaries; but it was to grow much more virulent in the 1920s and 1930s. One reason why it existed with so little challenge is that very few of Connolly's contemporaries actually subjected Catholic attitudes to the careful and detached analysis which he made, radical though their thought was in other respects. Many of them made radical observations on Catholicism, e.g. Joyce, or radical criticisms of it, e.g. Francis Sheehy-Skeffington; but few systematic examinations were made.

As to Chesterton and Belloc, our awareness of their anti-Semitism should certainly not blind us to the excellence of their work in other respects. Chesterton's anti-Semitism is well presented, for instance, in his short story 'The Quick One' in *The Scandal of Father Brown,* and I have been assisted by discussions on this question with Father Ian Boyd, who is preparing a thesis at the University of Aberdeen on Chesterton's social thought. A characteristic anti-Semitic effusion of Belloc is at hand in the poem on the Jewish financiers and the Boer war, printed in Randolph S. Churchill, *Winston S. Churchill,* II, London 1967. If any admirers of Chesterton and Belloc are pained by this information, let them remember Belloc's preface to his *The Bad Child's Book of Beasts:* 'Your little hands were meant to take the better things, and leave the worse ones' and apply this principle to their ideas. Belloc and Chesterton were outstanding in their denunciation of the Dublin employers of 1913. Mr Desmond Greaves has particularly stressed the acuteness of Belloc's analysis of the situation at that time, and enthusiastically quotes his paper, the *New Witness*. Desmond Ryan underlined Chesterton's poem, 'A Song of Swords', written in the same connection, with its biting lines directed at the Dublin capitalists:

> You gave the good Irish blood to grease
> The clubs of your country's enemies.
> You saw the brave man beat to his knees
> And you saw that it was good!

(Greaves, *Life of Connolly*, 247; Ryan, *Connolly*, 78–9.)

[10] Ryan, ed., *The Workers' Republic*, 264.

[11] 'Wee Joe Devlin' in Ryan, ed., *Socialism and Nationalism*, 83. The article initially appeared in *The Workers' Republic*, 28 Aug. 1915.

[12] 'Mr John E. Redmond, M.P.: His Strength and Weakness' in Ryan, ed., *Socialism and Nationalism*, 78. The essay first appeared in *Forward*, 18 March 1911.

[13] The reader may express surprise that in an essay where so much attention is paid to Connolly's intellectual relations with Catholicism I have not alluded more to Father Kane, and the great reply to him in 'Labour, Nationality and Religion'. First, I would hope that that pamphlet will be read in its entirety, and no synopsis could do it justice. Secondly, the printed word sometimes clouds the nature of a historical event; we are in danger of placing too much significance in Father Kane because Connolly apparently went to such lengths to refute him. In fact, Father Kane, who was stone blind, had much less impact on his times than the reprint of his sermons or Connolly's answer to them might suggest, and the major importance of 'Labour, Nationality and Religion' is of course the degree to which Connolly was simply using the occasion of Father Kane's sermons to make some major positive analyses of his own.

[14] Elizabeth Gurley Flynn has a dramatic description of a speech in Italian by Connolly to an Italian working-class audience in the U.S.A. in her *I Speak My Own Piece*.

[15] Mr Greaves particularly stresses the influence on Connolly of Schaffle's hostile but comparatively sound exposition of Socialism (*Life of Connolly*, 37).

[16] 'Father Finlay, S.J., and Socialism' in Ryan, ed., *The Workers' Republic*, 39–43, a piece originally appearing in *The Workers' Republic*, 1 July 1899.

[17] Sidney Gifford Czira ('John Brennan') recalled one amusing case of a man at Connolly's meetings in Dublin who 'had a frightful poisonous hatred against all Catholic clergy, and in fact I think the Catholic religion, and the beginning of his speech would often be like this: "What are the three greatest curses that came into this country? Christianity, the Catholic church and—" . . . I don't know what the other one was. Connolly got a bit weary of this and he got up and said, "Comrade, I don't know what the three greatest curses were, but the first one is yourself." ' (From Ó Gallchoir prod., *On Behalf of the Provisional Government*, no. 4, 'James Connolly'.) See also Ryan, *Connolly*, 36–37.

[18] Desmond Ryan was in very many ways representative of the Connolly generation, and it seems to me that his attitude to the question of clericalism and anti-clericalism, as sensitively explored by Conor Cruise O'Brien, testifies to the gulf which lay between the intellectual freedom and healthy fastidiousness of the Connolly generation, and the bitter controversies on the theme after the Civil War:

> Desmond Ryan, I think, found the whole subject distasteful; neither the thunderings of political priests nor the ingrowing bitterness of many Irish 'anti-clericals' could impress or attract such a mind as his, and the general pawing around of spiritual things which such controversy involves must have hurt him. Several of his anecdotes suggest also that he considered the controversy not only unseemly but also politically irrelevant: 'the influence of the priests' being often merely an excuse for the cowardice of the laity. (Cruise O'Brien, reviewing Desmond Ryan, *The Fenian Chief*, in *The Listener*, 7 March 1968.)

Naturally one does not wish to overstrain the analogy between Ryan's attitudes and those of the Connolly generation. Few men possess Desmond Ryan's aesthetic balance. The attitudes for which he had so much distaste were present before 1916 as well as afterwards; the Ryan mentality and its antithesis (either passionate clericalism or anti-clericalism) could co-exist in a single mind. But I do suggest that Desmond Ryan's view was the prevailing one among the intellectual leaders of the Connolly generation, and that it became much less common in the 1920s and 1930s.

[19] Connolly to the editor, *Catholic Times*, 8 Nov. 1912, quoted in Ryan, *Connolly*, 41. Connolly was replying to an attack on his 'Labour, Nationality and Religion' by the Rev. John MacErlean, S.J. See the *Catholic Times* also for 18 Oct., 18 Nov., and (for Connolly's final rebuttal) 22 Nov. 1912.

[20] Nora Connolly O'Brien, in Ó Gallchoir prod., *Provisional Government*, no. 4, 'Connolly'.

[21] 'He published a monthly magazine called *The Harp*. It was a pathetic sight to see him standing, poorly clad, at the door of the Cooper Union in New York or some other East Side hall, selling his little paper. None of the prosperous professional Irish, who shouted their admiration for him after his death, lent him a helping hand at this time.' (Flynn, *I Speak My Own Piece*, quoted in Ó Gallchoir prod., *Provisional Government*, no. 4, 'Connolly'.)

[22] *The Harp* (Jan. 1908).

[23] In this context, I find the insight of the poet Peter Levi, S.J., to be very indicative of the similarity of Connolly and Thomas More in their attitude to truth—at once enquiring, receptive, seeking an increase in knowledge through increase of intellectual encounter, and ready to die for it. I refer particularly to these words of Father Levi:

> Wisdom is justified in its children.
> Truth is scribbled on water, it breaks like bone,
> what Thomas suffered is written in stone.
> His wisdom was not in earthquake and fire,
> it was like the persistent, whistling air.

Thomas loved truth, not dragged it by the hair,
he said variety of opinion
would be of one mind in the world to come.

(Peter Levi, S.J., 'Sermon on St Thomas More' in *The Tablet*, 24 Aug. 1968.)

[24] Following the agenda for future study on such points which Connolly left us, Professor Patrick Lynch has provided an estimate of Thompson in the light of modern historical research: see his essay in Boyle, ed., *Leaders and Workers*. Michael Viney re-examined Ralahine in several articles which appeared in the *Irish Times* of 23, 24 and 25 May under the title 'The Commune of Clare'.

[25] John A. Ryan, D.D., *The Church and Interest-Taking: A Study Suggested by Wilhelm Hohoff's Book: 'Die Bedeutung der Marx'schen Kapitalkritik'*, St Louis, Mo., and Freiburg (Baden), 1910, being the reprint of an article in the *Catholic Fortnightly Review*. See also Ryan 'The Moral Aspect of Stockwatering' in *American Ecclesiastical Review*, Feb. and June, 1909. Information on Hohoff is derived from German biographical dictionaries and library catalogues. I am exceedingly obliged to Professor Lynch for drawing to my attention and lending me Ryan's very rare pamphlet: indeed, the whole appendix follows lines of investigation suggested by him.

[26] Ryan, *Church and Interest-Taking*, 3. I have restored the correct text, which was accidentally corrupted by a printing error involving the transposition of lines.

[27] See article on 'The State' in *New Catholic Encyclopedia*, for passing reference to Hohoff's rejection of the withering-away.

[28] Ryan, *Church and Interest-Taking*, 30, 31, 38, quoting Slater, *Irish Ecclesiastical Record* (Feb. 1909), 141, and Harty, *Irish Theological Quarterly* (Oct. 1907), 435. The volume quoted by Dom Aidan Gasquet (afterwards Cardinal) is his *Christian Democracy in Pre-Reformation Times*. The relevance of all this Catholic re-examination of the past in the light of modern economics will naturally recall the work of Max Weber and R. H. Tawney to students; Hohoff seems to have a place in both of their traditions.

CHAPTER 3

[1] Connolly, 'A Continental Revolution', 15 Aug. 1914, in Ryan, ed., *Labour and Easter Week*, 40.

[2] 'India is regarded by its alien rulers as a huge human cattle farm to be worked solely in the interest of the dominant nation. Whatever is done for its vast internal resources, is done for the benefit of the Indian people, but primarily with a view to the dividends which the investing classes of England may draw from such development.' Connolly in the Limerick *Leader*, July 1897, quoted in Ryan, ed., *Labour and Easter Week 1916*, note to 'British and Russian Imperialism', p. 33. See also Connolly's resolution of sympathy with the Boer Republics adopted at a Dublin public meeting, 27 Aug. 1899, of which one clause read: 'Whereas there were in India, Egypt and other portions of the British Empire other and much larger populations [than that of Ireland] also kept down in forced subjection', reprinted in Ryan, ed., *Labour and Easter Week*, 30. Mr Greaves also points to 'two well-documented articles' in *The Harp* in 1908 entitled 'The Coming Revolt in India' (Greaves, *Life of Connolly*, 181).

[3] Greaves, *Life of Connolly*, 338 and note.

[4] Ryan, 'James Connolly' in Boyle, ed., *Leaders and Workers*, 67.

[5] The classic, artistic and wholly individual critique of 1916 by O'Casey appears in the latter part of his *Drums Under the Windows*. But see also his *The Story of the Irish Citizen Army*, Dublin 1919, signed 'P. Ó Cathasaigh', and Greaves, *Life of Connolly*, 299. Dr Edward MacLysaght supplies some interesting background material in his contribution to Martin, ed., *Leaders and Men*, and I am most happy to have had a talk with Mr Greaves on the matter in the light of his own discussions with O'Casey.

[6] Connolly, 'A Continental Revolution', in *Forward*, 15 Aug. 1914, reprinted in Ryan, ed., *Labour and Easter Week*, 38–42, the passage quoted being from p. 39.

[7] Donal Nevin, 'James Connolly 1868–1916', Thomas Davis Lecture. Mr Nevin has most generously made his text available to me.

⁸I have not, unfortunately, had the pleasure of reading Dr Thornley's remarks in their original form, but they are quoted verbatim by Mr Nevin in his Thomas Davis lecture. The passage in question reads: [Connolly was a Marxist leader] 'applying with complete logic Marxist teaching on the proper tactics for the proletariat in the context of imperialist war'. If, of course, Dr Thornley is merely alluding to Connolly's specific articles teaching insurgent warfare, notably those reprinted by New Books Publications in James Connolly, *Revolutionary Warfare*, then I beg his pardon; but his language seems a little superlative and its meaning would seem to relate to the entire context of Connolly's path to insurrection.

⁹Michael O'Riordan, 'Introduction' in Connolly, *Revolutionary Warfare*, vi.

¹⁰Mr Kolpakov's articles have appeared in various Soviet Historical publications; it is to be hoped that a book and its English translation are in progress as far as he is concerned. On the Ceannt-Griffith confrontation see Ryan, *Connolly*, 75–6, and Greaves, *Life of Connolly*, 221. To my regret, I cannot now thank Cathal O'Shannon for a most helpful discussion on Mac Diarmada's attitude to Socialism, based on his own personal knowledge and wide research; his death has severed a most valuable link with Connolly's generation. Mr Nevin in his Thomas Davis lecture made the point that direct trade union support for the Irish Citizen Army was less widespread than was the readiness of trade unionists to take part in the Irish Volunteers; in particular he mentions 'two outstanding trade union leaders who were killed in the Rising, Richard O'Carroll, a member of the national executive of the Irish T.U.C., and Peadar Macken, the vice-president of the Dublin Trades Council, [both of whom] were in the Irish Volunteers, not in Connolly's Citizen Army'.

¹¹Archie Heron, in Ó Gallchoir prod., *Provisional Government*, no. 4, 'Connolly'.

¹²I have worked out the interaction of these nationalist strands in more detail in my 'Irish Nationalism', in Owen Dudley Edwards, Gwynfor Evans, Ioan Rhys and Hugh

MacDiarmid, *Celtic Nationalism*, London 1968, 126–33, 154–7, 178–203.

[13] Nobody has demonstrated more effectively than Desmond Ryan how vital a symbol Clarke was in that period. See his *Remembering Sion*, and also his 'Stephens, Devoy, Tom Clarke', in Cruise O'Brien, ed., *Shaping of Modern Ireland*, whence comes the quotation from *Paradise Lost*.

[14] 'Physical Force in Irish Politics', in Ryan, ed., *Socialism and Nationalism*, 55–6, a piece first published on 22 July 1899.

[15] 'A Continental Revolution', in Ryan, ed., *Labour and Easter Week*, 42.

[16] 'Can Warfare be Civilised?', in Ryan, ed., *Labour and Easter Week*, 50.

[17] 'A War for Civilisation', in Ryan, ed., *Labour and Easter Week*, 90, a piece first published on 30 Oct. 1915.

[18] Maureen Wall, 'The Background to the Rising; from 1914 until the issue of the countermanding order on Easter Saturday, 1916', in Kevin B. Nowlan, ed., *The Making of 1916—Studies in the History of the Rising*, Dublin 1969, 167.

[19] Maureen Wall, 'The Plans and the Countermand: the Country and Dublin' in Nowlan, *Making of 1916*, 227; G. A. Hayes-McCoy, 'A Military History of the 1916 Rising', *ibid.*, 294.

[20] 'A Continental Revolution', in Ryan, ed., *Labour and Easter Week*, 39–40.

[21] 'Can Warfare be Civilised?', in Ryan, ed., *Labour and Easter Week*, 54.

[22] Wall, 'The Plans and the Countermand' in Nowlan, ed., *Making of 1916*, 225–7.

[23] *Ibid.*, 222–3.

[24] Walter Kendall, *The Revolutionary Movement in Britain 1900–21—The Origins of British Communism*, London 1969, 71. Greaves, *Life of Connolly*, 134–84. But this episode needs further study. Greaves, on such a question, reads too much post-1917 doctrinaire interpretation into the matter, deeply diligent a researcher though he is. Kendall has also some depth in research but his work is warped by hostility to its subject. On Connolly's short way with nomenclature and

hence *amour-propre* for organisations, see Kendall, 21: 'It does not matter what you call yourself, you'll be dubbed the Socialist Labour Party anyway' said he of the party which in the event took that name when he made the point in Edinburgh, June 1903.

CHAPTER 4

[1] Connolly, *The Re-Conquest of Ireland*, with an introduction by A. Raftery, Dublin and Belfast 1968, 67. The pamphlet was published in 1915 but its main content was written in 1911 and 1912.

[2] *Remembering Sion*, 179.

[3] Nora Connolly O'Brien, in Ó Gallchoir prod., *Provisional Government*, no. 4, 'Connolly'. A very moving sketch of Skeffington's life and death is that by his son Owen in Edwards and Pyle, ed., *1916*. This is the best account, but see also Roger MacHugh, 'Tom Kettle and Frank Sheehy-Skeffington' in Cruise O'Brien, ed., *Shaping of Modern Ireland*.

[4] Ryan, *Connolly*, 133–34, reprints a large segment of the critique.

[5] With an introduction by F. S. L. Lyons, London 1967.

[6] Professor Lyons in his introduction suggests that he had, but this seems an unduly static interpretation of Skeffington's intellectual development. A close reading of *Michael Davitt* suggests that Skeffington then regarded himself as ready to endorse violence under some circumstances, and cited Tolstoy as the unpalatable extreme as regards questions of peace and war.

Connolly's review appeared in *The Harp* (Aug. 1908).

[7] Mr Ailfrid Mac Lochlainn drew my attention to this letter which is preserved in the National Library of Ireland. It is dated 5 April 1911 and the recipient's first name is 'Maurice'.

[8] Greaves, *Life of Connolly*, 299. The files of Skeffington's *Irish Citizen* indicate the vast range of his social attitudes and many interesting points of contact are to be seen in the papers edited by the two men.

[9] Connolly to William O'Brien, 12 September 1909, printed in William O'Brien, *Forth the Banners Go*, ed. Edward MacLysaght, Dublin 1969, 239–40.

[10] O'Brien, *Forth the Banners Go*, 16.

[11] Connolly, *Re-Conquest of Ireland*, 43–4, 48.

[12] Connolly, 'Can Warfare be Civilised?' in Ryan, ed., *Labour and Easter Week*, 54.

[13] Wall, 'The Plans and the Countermand' in Nowlan, ed., *Making of 1916*, 224. See also Brian Farrell's useful essay 'Markievicz and the Women of the Revolution' in Martin, ed., *Leaders and Men of the Easter Rising*, 227–38.

[14] O'Brien, *Forth the Banners Go*, 106.

[15] There is extraordinary discrepancy in primary and secondary source-material concerning this body. What we have are statements from survivors, notably William O'Brien and Seán T. O'Kelly, describing a meeting which took place in the Library of the Gaelic League on 9 September 1914. According to the O'Kelly version, this meeting took the decision to stage an insurrection in Ireland during the war. O'Brien largely supports this, but, points out Desmond Greaves, his list of 'those present . . . differs so much from O'Kelly's that it is best to assume that the two men described different meetings of a series' (Greaves, *Life of Connolly*, 290 fn.) and it also seems reasonable to assume that in a situation where an 'open organisation', viz., the Irish Neutrality League, and a secret group, involving some, but not all of the open group's leaders, were constantly meeting, recollections of who was where became confused. Clearly, Skeffington was not in the secret group. But equally clearly, the Irish Neutrality League had some secret proceedings at which tactics were worked out as to how best to carry through non-violent action. Hence yet further confusion in the recollection of survivors.

[16] Greaves, *Life of Connolly*, 291–2; O'Brien, introduction to *Labour and Easter Week*, ed. Ryan, 3–5; Wall, 'Background to the Rising' in Nowlan, ed., *Making of 1916*, 166–7, whence comes the 'last man' quotation. Mrs Wall (*ibid.*, 168) cites an earlier case, from Boer War days, of Connolly's allegedly

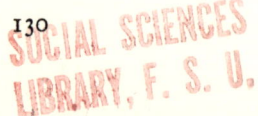

advocating seizure of buildings as commencement of the proclamation of a Republic. The story emanates from Arthur Griffith, who stated that Connolly confided the idea to him, or rather from George Lyons' recollection of Griffith's statement. The whole thing seems most improbable; the racist and anti-Socialist Griffith would hardly have been Connolly's choice as a recipient of such drastic confidences. 'The story of a long intimate connection between Connolly and Griffith is completely apocryphal' (Greaves, *Life of Connolly*, 94). Because Connolly took certain actions in 1916, certain gentlemen found it easy to convince themselves he was perpetually on the boil to similar purpose. I know of one old gentleman who maintains that Connolly and he proposed to seize Edinburgh Castle in 1913; presumably in order to divert attention from the Dublin Lock-out. Connolly had a sense of humour, and it is probable, to put the matter charitably, that some light reference was recalled as evidence of long-cherished plans.

[17] An interesting view of Connolly's slowness in moving to absolutely physical force solutions is given by Mr Donal O'Connor Lysaght in his 'Connolly, Syndicalism and Irish Labour', an introduction to Connolly, *Socialism Made Easy*, Dublin 1968, 8. The thought-provoking character of some of his speculations must not be ignored, despite his rather condescending tone and the offensive remarks he permits himself, impugning the integrity of Desmond Ryan as editor of Connolly's works; as far as integrity is concerned, there are few worthy to loose the latchet of Desmond Ryan's shoes. For Skeffington's growing fears about militarism see particularly his 'Open Letter to Thomas MacDonagh' reprinted in Edwards and Pyle, ed., *1916: The Easter Rising*, 149; also Greaves, *Life of Connolly*, 299, 310.

[18] O'Brien, introduction to Ryan, ed., *Labour and Easter Week*, 20.

[19] Laughter is normally one of the first qualities to elude the search of the historian. It is, normally, preserved only in the recollection of contemporaries, and piety frequently decrees its elimination from the official record, or else serves it up

in a pallid and canned fashion. Fortunately, Owen Sheehy-Skeffington's recollection has preserved most faithfully the humanity as well as the greatness of his father; interested students would also do well to turn to Skeffington's more imaginative propaganda writings which appeared in his newspaper.

CHAPTER 5

[1] Connolly, on being asked by a priest before his execution to pray for his executioners. (See Greaves, *Life of Connolly*, 339-40.)

[2] I would like to acknowledge my intellectual obligations in the making of this lecture to three of the essays in Edwards and Pyle, ed., *1916*, which have not been cited here. Donal McCartney's 'Gaelic Ideological Origins' offers an interpretation of the Connolly generation as a whole as far as a major factor in ideology is concerned; R. Dudley Edwards, in 'The Achievement of 1916', raises some critical questions respecting continuities and breaks in the transmission of a legacy from the insurrection; and Conor Cruise O'Brien's 'The Embers of Easter' is a statement of the relations between contemporary Ireland and the Easter Rising which has obviously influenced my remarks here to a very considerable degree.